HOPE
Prevails

BIBLE STUDY

INSIGHTS FROM A DOCTOR'S PERSONAL JOURNEY
Through Depression

BIBLE STUDY

INSIGHTS FROM A DOCTOR'S PERSONAL JOURNEY
Through Depression

DR. MICHELLE BENGTSON

Published by Redemption Press, PO Box 427, Enumclaw, WA 98022

Toll Free (844) 2REDEEM (273-3336)

Redemption Press is honored to present this title in partnership with the author. The views expressed or implied in this work are those of the author. Redemption Press provides our imprint seal representing design excellence, creative content, and high quality production.

Unless otherwise indicated, all Bible quotations are from the *Holy Bible, New International Version*®, *NIV*®Copyright ©1973, 1978, 1984, 2011 by Biblica, Inc.® Used by permission. All rights reserved worldwide.

Scriptures marked (KJV) are taken from the King James Version of the Bible (KJV).

Scriptures marked (MSG) are taken from The Message (MSG), copyright © 1993, 1994, 1995, 1996, 2000, 2001, 2002 by Eugene H. Peterson.

Scriptures marked (NLT) are taken from the Holy Bible, New Living Translation, copyright © 1996, 2004, 2015 by Tyndale House Foundation. Used by permission of Tyndale House Publishers Inc., Carol Stream, Illinois 60188. All rights reserved.

ISBN-13: 978-1-68314-253-9
        978-1-68314-254-6 (ePub)
        978-1-68314-255-3 (Mobi)

Library of Congress Catalog Card Number: 2017946423

CONTENTS

PRAISE FOR THE HOPE PREVAILS BIBLE STUDY

The *Hope Prevails Bible Study* is like having your own personal psychologist leading you through the tangled thoughts of a depressed person. The insightful and probing questions allow the reader to unwrap those thoughts, exposing them to the light. It offers practical exercises, which, when followed, can open up doors to understand and healing depression. Dr. Bengtson understands the tyranny of depression because she was once severely depressed herself. She approaches this subject matter not only as a doctor, but also as one who's been there. She does it with easy-to-understand language, with compassion, and with wisdom. Unlike many doctors who treat only the physical, mental, and emotional aspects of this condition, Dr. Bengtson has the courage to also address the spiritual aspect. She does it masterfully, having discovered the importance of the spiritual component in any healing scenario.

Peg Bradley, author, *The Tree: When Pride Takes a Fall*

Dr. Michelle Bengtson has done it again. The *Hope Prevails Bible Study* delivers the same great authentic connection, raw insights, and powerful truths that we received from her book *Hope Prevails: Insights from a Doctor's Personal Journey through Depression*. Having been in church ministry for many years, and now a lead pastor, I see this study not only as a great resource for individuals, but as highly beneficial to both church and counseling groups.

Dr. Bengtson is not just a neuropsychologist; she is a person who has also experienced the journey from depression to mental health. Her experiences allow her to uniquely sympathize with people in the midst of depression. The *Hope Prevails Bible Study* combines her experiences and knowledge in order to infuse strength and hope into anyone who participates in it.

Pastor Debbie Kitterman, founder of Dare 2 Hear Ministry
International Speaker and Author, *Releasing God's Heart
through Hearing His Voice*

Dr. Michelle Bengtson has a gift for sharing her vulnerability through her personal battle with depression. Using her personal and professional experience, Dr. Bengtson bridges the gap between hope and despair for her readers and leads them straight to the heart of God, where healing can begin. This Bible study is beautifully crafted as a companion or independent resource to *Hope Prevails* and is an invaluable resource essential to any library.

Donna Hughes

Prior to reading *Hope Prevails: Insights from a Doctor's Personal Journey through Depression,* I was always at a loss as to what to say to someone held in the grip of depression. Nor was I equipped to handle my own moments of deep insecurity and pain. Reading *Hope Prevails* gave me a better understanding of depression and how it affects a person's entire being—mind, body, and soul. But it was when I worked through the *Hope Prevails Bible Study,* taking the time to really look inside my own heart and beliefs, that I gained a greater awareness of how deep the spiritual roots of depression truly run. This Bible study helped reveal in my own life an awareness that I am not immune to believing many of the lies of the enemy that keep me from truly seeing myself as God sees me. Though I may never have been given a diagnosis of depression by a doctor, I need to do the work contained in the pages of the *Hope Prevails Bible Study* to be set free from strongholds in my life that have held me captive for far too long. And I truly believe that the truths from God's Word that are presented in this Bible study can set you free, as well!

Gina Kelly

Dr. Bengtson takes our hand, as she promises, and walks us out of the lies that the enemy has whispered in our ears—sometimes for our whole lives—that have led to our depression, self-doubt, and brokenness. Having learned for herself, through many storms and trials, that He is always our healing path and ultimate answer, she gently and skillfully applies God's truth to wounded places of the heart. Her vulnerable personal stories, along with her doctor's perspective, let us know she's been there, too, and that she knows what she's talking about. The questions lead us to delve into the Word of God and do the work we need to do for our own healing to begin.

Mary Lee Morgan

The *Hope Prevails Bible Study* is so very timely. May God use it to take His people deeper into His Word and release them from the bondage of depression.

Ray Comfort, evangelist,
founder, Living Waters Publications

It's impossible to overstate how much Dr. Michelle Bengtson's *Hope Prevails Bible Study* has meant to me. The Bible study is a companion for her book, *Hope Prevails.* I'm a mentor, and both works have been invaluable tools in leading women to understand the roots of depression, their true identity, and the very certain hope that they can return to a life filled with joy and purpose. Few medical professionals love as well or put themselves in as vulnerable a position in order to help others find freedom from the torment of depression. Dr. Bengtson walks you step by step through the healing process, while addressing your spirit, soul, and body. Hope prevails because God and His Word always will. So pull up a chair, pick up your Bible, and prepare to be understood and made whole.

Cindy Miller, Women's Mentoring Leadership Team,
Gateway Church

As a huge fan of the book *Hope Prevails*, I was excited to hear that Dr. Bengtson was releasing a companion Bible study. Both are unique in a couple of ways. First, Dr. Michelle's personal view of depression, as a clinician and as one who has suffered from severe depression herself, gives credence to her message. Second, her focus on the spiritual roots of depression, as well as its chemical and genetic components, is something I've never seen in a book on depression before.

The Bible study takes us even deeper than the book (which is very comprehensive in itself). Answering each chapter's questions will be powerful in a group study. As former Freedom in Christ directors, my husband and I know that many people suffer from depression within the Church. We've also experienced the truth of the exhortation of James 5:16 (KJV): "Confess your faults one to another, and pray one for another, that ye may be healed" (KJV). Since pain shared is always pain lessened, I know that this Bible study, used in a group setting will be life transforming and sure to bring healing to many.

I highly recommend the *Hope Prevails Bible Study* as a companion to the book or as a stand-alone study.

Patricia Krank, speaker, former director at
Freedom Session International

This is a powerful Bible study filled with insight into becoming free from depression. Certainly Dr. Michelle Bengtson has addressed areas of hopelessness that can become fatal to a believer and their faith in God. Her transparency gives hope and the tools to step into a transformed life. I highly recommend the *Hope Prevails Bible Study* to individuals, church groups, small group Bible studies, or counseling groups everywhere.

Jan Aderholt, Ph.D., speaker, teacher, music artist

There was a time after our boys were born when my wife struggled with anxiety, panic attacks, and an increased heart rate. In time, she found herself fighting off depression daily, resulting in visits to the best cardiologists and neurologists. But none of them could find anything physically wrong. After nearly two years of immense struggles, we were introduced to a biblical teaching like *Hope Prevails*. I am so thankful that the Lord is moving on the hearts and minds of authors like Dr. Michelle Bengtson to address medical and emotional ailments with Scripture. Dr. Michelle has combined her amazing academic training and biblical revelation to produce a lifesaving book and now the *Hope Prevails Bible Study*. This resource should be required reading for anyone struggling with depression and for all ministry personnel. It not only offers wonderful information and revelation, but the thing I love most about it is that the focus is on Scripture and the healing work of the Holy Spirit. Dr. Michelle does a masterful job of engaging the reader and leading them to the healing waters that only Jesus can offer.

Stephen Emerick, executive senior pastor ,
Embassy City Church, Irving, Texas

There are numerous books on depression, but what has been missing is a solid Bible study on this topic. Truthfully, I wish *Hope Prevails*—both the book and the Bible study—had been available when I walked through my dark night of the soul. Dr. Bengtson combines her training, knowledge, and wisdom to gently take us to the only place we can find healing—God and His Word. She provides authentic stories from her own journey, insightful questions, and a doctor's perspective on biblical emotional health. The *Hope Prevails Bible Study* is a prescription not just to learn to survive, but to overcome the unwelcome stronghold of depression. You won't be disappointed. It is an excellent study for a small group or a one-on-one conversation.

Cynthia Cavanaugh, speaker, author of *Live Unveiled: Freedom to Worship God, Love Others, and Tell Your Story*

Dr. Michelle Bengtson has written the *Hope Prevails Bible Study* not only from a neuropsychologist's point of view, but also from a woman's heart—as someone who has personally walked out of the dark valley of depression by trusting God even when He seemed far away.

As a pastor's wife and mentor, I am thrilled for this material to use as a guide to help others who find themselves on the same journey that Dr. Bengtson writes of. This study will benefit not only those who are going through depression, but also those who are walking alongside those who are personally experiencing depression.

Every home around the world is touched in some way by anxiety and depression. The information and insight contained in this Bible study is material that God can use to bring deliverance and restoration.

Norma Miller, speaker, mentor, pastor's Wife,
Northside Church, Texarkana, Texas

I have known Dr. Bengtson for several years. I love her writings. Being a pastor, I appreciate her biblical perspective. I refer many people whom I counsel to her book, and now with the companion Bible study, this is a grand slam for God!!!! I have never seen so many people looking for hope in my time as a pastor as I do now, and Dr. Michelle answers that need of so very many, giving pastors another resource.

Pastor Dewey Moede, founder
For God's Glory Alone Ministries

When someone is willing to share their story from struggle to healing, I can't help but connect to them in my journey! Reading Dr. Michelle's book brought many "ME TOO!" moments from my own struggles with depression and my restoration.

I am delighted that Michelle is bringing us the "now what" in the form of this wonderful Bible study! This study helps provide insight to our own healing journey and takes us from hurting to healing! I love the reflective questions and key thoughts, which help bring everything together. The worshipful playlist also helps shift the focus onto our Creator! Be ready to be transformed!

Polly Hamp
Author, NLP practitioner, Freedom coach

Freedom. Isn't that why someone sees a neuropsychologist—to be freed of what torments them?

Combine that freedom with a Bible study, and imagine the power when Jesus is the Healer. That's what Dr. Michelle Bengtson addresses in the *Hope Prevails Bible Study*: the whole person—the physical, emotional, AND spiritual health of the reader.

Whether you are dealing with depression or another physical, emotional or spiritual stronghold, I heartily recommend "what the Doctor orders" in *Hope Prevails*!

Susan B. Mead, founder of His Girls Gather

A PRAYER AS YOU BEGIN

Dear heavenly Father,

You know the heart and the needs of the one who has picked up the *Hope Prevails Bible Study* and now holds it in their hands. Even Jesus asked the lame man if he wanted to get well, in part because He knew that true healing often requires effort on our part. Father, it is *not* Your will that any of Your children suffer from depression. In fact, You say in Your Word that it is Your desire that we would be in health and prosper, even as our soul prospers. So, Father, as Your precious child begins to do the work of reading this book and answering the questions in this Bible study, I ask that You would illuminate lies that do not align with Your truth, that You would bring comfort and healing to the broken places, and that the bondage of depression would be broken so that joy could return in the morning. Because of and in the name of Jesus, I pray. Amen.

INTRODUCTION

I attended more years of school than I want to count. There is one thing that I learned: When I actually read the texts, studied the lecture notes and assigned reading, and did the work, I learned the material so much better than when I just sat in class or skimmed the reading. The courses in which I fully invested myself are those I remember the most today, decades later.

Another thing I know to be true: There was a reason Jesus asked the lame man if he wanted to get well. He knew that (1) getting well would require some work on the lame man's part, and (2) He knew that being well would be an adjustment for the man. He would have to assimilate himself into society and discard the labels, habits, and coping mechanisms he had grown accustomed to for all those years. He had a choice to make: Did he want to be well badly enough to be willing to do the work?

I regularly see this issue in my office. Patients come in, undergo an evaluation, and then receive a diagnosis and prescription for treatment. Frequently, however, patients leave with prescription and treatment plan in hand and then never follow through, only to return a year or two later in worse shape than when they originally came in. Why? Because they weren't willing to do the work. One can only assume they didn't really want to get well, although they said they did when they first walked in my door.

So the question I pose to you as you crack open this Bible study is this: Do you want to get well? If your answer is yes, then I encourage you to do the work. Pray and ask God to reveal what He has for you between the covers of *Hope Prevails: Insights from a Doctor's Personal Journey through Depression* and this study written as a complement to *Hope Prevails*. You can do the Bible study alone, but it'll be more impactful if you go through it as you read *Hope Prevails*.

If you want to get the most from this Bible study, I recommend you read the original book, *Hope Prevails*, on which this study is based, then listen to the playlists, read the prayers as if they were written just for you, take time to memorize the verses in the Your Rx sections, and answer the questions throughout. You'll find that these in-depth questions will help you pinpoint where you are and how to get where you want to go.

I wrote *Hope Prevails* to share the comfort that God gave me when I was in the valley of depression, when I needed to know I wasn't alone and there was a way out. God helped me through it. The Bible tells us that He is no respecter of persons, which means that He doesn't play favorites. If He did that for me, He will do it for you, as well.

So let's start this journey out of the valley together—you've been there long enough!

Because of Him, hope prevails!
(Dr.) Michelle Bengtson

WHEN THE WHOLE WORLD IS LAUGHING BUT YOU

"For I know the plans I have for you," declares the LORD,
"plans to prosper you and not to harm you, plans to give
you hope and a future."
Jeremiah 29:11

To someone who is going through hardship or heartache, two of the most comforting words anyone can say is, "Me, too!"

"Me, too" welcomes you into a community. It breathes life back into a sagging soul. It breeds acceptance where feelings of rejection linger. It kicks isolation to the curb. It gives you a hand to hold and a heart to beat with you.

We can face any difficulty with greater determination and strength if we believe we are not alone in the fight. Unfortunately, when I walked through my own valley of depression, it felt like the whole world was laughing but me. What I most longed for was for someone to come alongside me and say, "Me, too."

Part of the reason I wrote *Hope Prevails* and this Bible study was to assure you that you're not alone because I've been there. Even as the professional, the doctor with all the alphabet soup letters after my name, I wasn't immune to depression. I've gone through it and am on the other side now.

I want to share with you how I got here, and how you, too, can get to the other side. I want to dispel some of the lies and myths surrounding depression. And I want to offer hope, a hope that prevails.

Just hold on a little bit longer, take my hand, and walk through these pages with me. Together, we'll get to the other side. And depression will be a distant memory for you, as well.

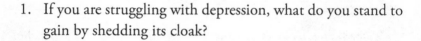

1. If you are struggling with depression, what do you stand to gain by shedding its cloak?

2. Hope was the thing that got me through my period of depression. For me, without hope I'd have no reason to live. How would you define or describe hope?

Key Thoughts ⟝

- Depression often feels like the whole world is laughing but you, but you are not alone.
- Someone else understands.
- Hope gives us a reason to keep going.

Recommended Playlist ⟝

Music helped me so much in my healing journey, so at the end of each chapter, just as in the original *Hope Prevails*, I will offer you a list of songs that I think will encourage you in your healing journey.

"Broken Vessels (Amazing Grace)," Hillsong Worship, © 2014 by Hillsong Church T/A Hillsong Music Australia
"The Best Days of My Life," Jason Gray, © 2014 by Centricity Music
"Walls," Cody Carnes, © 2012 by Gateway Create Publishing
"You Invite Me In," Meredith Andrews, © 2008 by Word Records

A LETTER TO MY DEPRESSED SELF

Who comforts us in all our troubles, so that we can comfort those in any trouble with the comfort we ourselves receive from God.

2 Corinthians 1:4

Time has a way of giving us perspective. As I've gotten older, experience and the wisdom that comes with age have shown that so many of the things I concerned myself with as a younger woman don't hold the importance I once thought they did. Have you ever looked back on a situation with awe and amazement at how you made it through or what God did during that time that you couldn't have known in the difficult moments?

A change in perspective can also be helpful. Have you ever received a card, e-mail, or text message of encouragement just when you needed it? That has happened to me on a couple of occasions, and when it did, it felt like a hug from heaven. I wanted to cry in gratitude because I knew God saw me and cared about me and my needs.

After the darkest stretch of my depression was behind me, God prompted me to write "A Letter to My Depressed Self."[1] Just like a well-timed note from a friend, this would serve as a form of encouragement for me on the other side of depression's valley should I ever start to see those dark clouds form again.

1. If you were to write a note of encouragement to a depressed friend, what would you say?

2. What encouragement do Romans 8:31, Philippians 4:19, and Psalm 121 offer?

3. Depression is not a punishment from God. When you're going through a hard time and want to give up, you must cling to the promise He gives in Jeremiah 29:11 that God knows the plans He has for you, "plans to _____ you and not to _____ you, plans to give you a _____ and a _____"(NIV).

Key Thoughts —◦

- God is for us and wants to meet our needs.
- Depression is not a punishment from God.
- God promises that His plans for you and your future are good.

Recommended Playlist —◦

"Tell Your Heart to Beat Again," Danny Gokey, © 2014 by BMG Rights Management

"Soar," Meredith Andrews, © 2016 by WordWorship/Word Music Publishing

"Still," Hillary Scott, © 2016 by HST Entertainment/EMI Records Nashville

"I Have This Hope," Tenth Avenue North, © 2016 by Provident Label Group LLC

Chapter 1

THIS THING CALLED DEPRESSION

I will be glad and rejoice in your love,
for you saw my affliction and knew the anguish of my soul.
Psalm 31:7

I love a perfectly manicured lawn: fresh-cut green grass, edged and lined with flowers or mulch. But have you ever had the experience where it seems like out of nowhere, your beautiful lawn has become a haven for weeds, where your once-lovely lawn is no longer recognizable as your own because of the troublesome intruders that have taken up residence and made it unsightly?

Like a lawn overrun by weeds, depression often has a way of sneaking up on us and taking us unaware. Sometimes we don't even recognize it in ourselves. Rather, friends or loved ones notice the signs and symptoms before we do. I grew up in a home with a depressed mother, and I had been a doctor for many years, diagnosing depression in patients. Yet when I first experienced depression myself, after the birth of our oldest child, I didn't recognize it for what it was.

When it was finally brought to my attention, I had mixed reactions. I first felt relief, because a diagnosis gave me hope that life would improve, but I also felt shame because I felt like I should've been able to prevent it or treat it on my own with the clinical knowledge I had. Depression deceives and colors our perception.

1. Read Hosea 4:6a. How does this verse apply to not seeing the signs of depression in ourselves and, therefore, not asking for help?

2. How often are you reluctant to ask yourself the hard questions because you don't want anyone to know you are struggling? Or do you find that you don't want to admit the answer even to yourself?

Keep in mind as you go through the pages of *Hope Prevails* and this Bible study, God already knows the answers to the questions you've been hesitant to ask, and He longs to bring help, hope, and healing to those places that have previously brought you only shame.

3. I related the description of depression to "like drown-
   ing except you can see everyone around you breathing."
   [2] How does David describe depression in Psalm 42:5;
   42:11; and 43:5?

   How would you describe depression?

4. While the central topic of *Hope Prevails* is depression, as
   you will see when we get deeper into this study, it's really
   about the lies from the enemy of our souls.
   Write out Isaiah 5:20 here:

   In my childhood home, depression was a way of life and
   my mother's depression was viewed as, "That's just the way
   she is."

   For reflection: What maladaptive styles do you see in your
   life that you didn't recognize for what they were?

5. Many people don't realize how prevalent depression is, or even that they themselves suffer from it. About one out of every four Americans will experience depression at some point in their lives. Also, nearly twice as many women as men are estimated to be affected by a depressive disorder each year. Does that surprise you?

6. Why do you think only 29 percent of all people with depression report contacting a mental health professional? What do you think are the greatest barriers to seeking help?

7. Put a check next to each symptom you've experienced for more than two weeks:
   - ❏ Feeling sad, blue, down, or numb
   - ❏ Irritability, agitation, or frustration
   - ❏ Concentration problems
   - ❏ Feelings of worthlessness, helplessness, and/or hopelessness
   - ❏ Feeling guilty
   - ❏ Trouble making decisions
   - ❏ Decline in energy/motivation
   - ❏ Decreased interest in previously enjoyed activities
   - ❏ Withdrawal/reduced social interaction
   - ❏ Crying
   - ❏ Disturbed sleep

❏ Disturbed appetite
❏ Unintentional weight gain or loss
❏ Aches and pains that do not improve despite treatment
❏ Excessive use of alcohol or other substances (including prescription medication)
❏ Suicidal thoughts

Did this surprise you? Why or why not?

8. Look up Psalm 31:7; Psalm 33:20; Psalm 34:17–18, Psalm 54:4, and Hebrews 13:6. What characteristic of God is offered as encouragement to us when we feel we can't make it on our own? How does that make you feel?

9. Write out Isaiah 41:13 here.

As you embark on this study, will you agree in your heart to surrender any fear and let God help you shed the shackles of depression?

Key Thoughts ⌁

- We hurt ourselves by being uninformed.
- Frequently, people don't recognize depression for what it is.
- God wants to be our help, even when we are depressed.

Your Rx ⌁

If you came to see me in my office, I'd give you a treatment plan, a prescription (Rx). Because you're largely doing the work (the treatment plan) by engaging in this study, the only additional recommendation I feel led to offer is that you look up the following verses: Psalm 31:7; Psalm 34:17–18, and Isaiah 41:13 in your preferred version of the Bible. Then write them out here on index cards and keep them where you will see them often. Read these verses aloud at least three times daily, committing them to memory.

The reason this is so important is because Scripture says that faith comes by hearing, and in our journey out of depression, we need to bolster our faith with God's truth.

Recommended Playlist ⌁

"Lift Up Your Head," Meredith Andrews, © 2008 by Word Records

"The River," Meredith Andrews, © 2008 by Word Records

"Never Miss a Beat," Natalie Grant, © 2015 by Curb Records, Inc.

"Find You Here," Ellie Holcomb, © 2017 by Full Heart Music

Chapter 2

YOU ARE NOT ALONE

For I wrote you out of great distress and anguish
of heart and with many tears,
not to grieve you but to let you know
the depth of my love for you.
2 Corinthians 2:4

"You're not alone. I understand."

Those are perhaps the two most comforting sentiments we long to hear in the midst of a trial. The opposite was what the enemy of my soul whispered in my ear so loudly it was deafening: *"You're all alone. No one else understands."*

The enemy made sure to use my own knowledge *and training against me: "You're the doctor. If you couldn't save yourself from such an affliction, why would anyone trust you to treat them? In fact, if anyone finds out, you'll lose business and become the laughingstock of your profession."* He wanted me to believe that my worth was dictated by my condition, and that I was flawed because I had walked in the valley.

The enemy is a liar—the father of lies, in fact. God's truth says that what the enemy intended to use to harm us, God will use for our good. It also says that we will be able to comfort others with the comfort that we have been given (2 Cor. 1:4).

In preparation for the release of *Hope Prevails*, I took a small group of women through the book with me in a book study format. At one point, one of the women messaged me and said, "THIS. Is. Me! You're telling my story for the past twenty-five years." But the not-so-strange part is that she wasn't the only one to share such sentiments with me. Many women have told me similar statements, yet each one has felt alone. And each, in her own way, has worn a mask, afraid to share her suffering, afraid to let anyone see her pain, afraid that no one else would understand.

It was my story, too. And it's the story of countless others. The enemy convinces so many of us that it is true—that they are alone and that no one else will understand. But I'm here to tell you that it is a lie. You are not alone. Someone does understand.

1. When depressed, it's tempting to feel alone. Record the assurances of Deuteronomy 31:8 and Joshua 1:9 here.

    Deuteronomy 31:8:

Joshua 1:9:

2. Even Christians get depressed. Why do you think Christians often feel they must hide their pain and pretend that nothing is wrong?

3. The Bible offers many promises for those who suffer through the torrent of depression. Record three of those promises here:

Matthew 5:4:

Psalm 126:5:

2 Corinthians 1:3–4:

Which did you find most comforting? Are there other scriptures that you find comforting for times of depression, despair, or grief?

4. "Dear friends, don't be surprised at the fiery trials you are
    going through, as if something strange were happening to
    you. Instead, be very glad—for these trials make you part-
    ners with Christ in his suffering, so that you will have the
    wonderful joy of seeing his glory when it is revealed to all
    the world" (1 Peter 4:12–13 NLT).

    What do you think this passage means when it says, "you
    will have the wonderful joy of seeing his glory when it is
    revealed to all the world" as it relates to your fiery trial?

5. Let's get real. Have you ever gone through a painful trial
    and felt stung or burned by the Christian platitudes or Bi-
    ble verses offered as the pat answer? Why didn't they help?

    What's the difference between those times and the times
    when Scripture *has* helped?

6. I went through a time when I was afraid that if I let myself cry, I might never stop. Have you ever felt that way?

What promise are we given in Psalm 56:8?

And in Revelation 21:4?

This is a safe time and place. This is a time ordained just for this. It's a time set aside for help and healing. You must feel it to heal it. And healing your hurts will dry your tears.

7. Read John 5:1–6. What did Jesus ask?

Why do you think He asked that question?

What do you think may be the biggest hindrance to people truly wanting to get well from their depression?

What hinders them from seeking healing in their life as a whole?

For reflection: Is there anything standing in *your* way?

8. You are not your depression. Any shame you feel does not come from God. What does Romans 8:1 say about Christ's followers?

9. Read Isaiah 51:11; Romans 15:1;, and 1 Peter 1:8. What is the common gift offered in these verses?

Key Thoughts ⌁
- You are not alone—many people struggle with depression, and most importantly, God is with you in this trial.
- God cares about your pain.
- You are not your depression, and shame does not come from God.
- Depression does not have to be a permanent part of your life. God wants to give us His joy.

Your Rx ⌁
Record the following verses on index cards, recite them at least three times daily, and commit them to memory: Deuteronomy 31:8; Matthew 5:4; Psalm 56:8; and Revelation 21:4.

Recommended Playlist ⌒

"Love Will Have the Final Word," Jason Gray, © 2014 by Centricity Music

"Trust in You," Lauren Daigle, © 2015 by Centricity Music

"Sovereign over Us," Aaron Keyes, © 2011 by Kingsway

"You're Not Alone," Meredith Andrews, © 2008 by Word Records

Chapter 3

THE UNDERLYING CAUSES OF DEPRESSION

Why, my soul, are you downcast?
Why so disturbed within me?
Put your hope in God,
for I will yet praise him,
my Savior and my God.
Psalm 42:5

You wouldn't have to spend much time with me to arrive at the conclusion that I not only have a sweet tooth, but I'm a self-proclaimed chocoholic. Add in a little sea-salt caramel, and we might become friends for life. Given the time, I enjoy cooking and baking. But I have found that you can give me a list of the ingredients in a dish, but that doesn't ensure I will be able to replicate it in my own kitchen.

Depression can happen very much the same way. There are chemical and genetic contributors; secondary contributors like physiology and medical disorders; reactionary contributors like environmental factors, major life changes, stress, and modeling within the home; and spiritual contributors to depression. Often, people experience several of these contributors at once. Yet not everyone's reaction to such contributors will lead to the same result.

All those contributors were likely a factor to some extent in my own experience with depression. Hormonal dysregulation following pregnancy contributed to postpartum symptoms. A thyroid disorder affected my mood, energy, and outlook. I am the product of a strong family history of depression, and my mother modeled a depressed outlook in the home. Graduate school, multiple moves, being a caregiver to a parent and a spouse with cancer, and miscarrying our baby were significant life stresses. Spiritually, I also battled the fear of rejection, fear of abandonment, self-hatred, self-pity, resentment, and unforgiveness. Someone else might deal with similar circumstances and not become depressed. For me, these things created the perfect storm.

1. While there are many contributors to depression, what do John 10:10; 1 Peter 5:8; and Ephesians 6:12 indicate are the primary contributors to our trials?

2. David vulnerably shares his pain with God in Psalm 42:5: "Why, my soul, are you downcast? Why so disturbed within me? Put your hope in God, for I will yet praise him, my Savior and my God." How do you praise God when you feel depressed and praise or thanksgiving seem like two of the most difficult things to do?

3. More than once, my husband has been diagnosed with cancer, and I've walked alongside him as his caregiver. Most of the time, asking why someone gets cancer is futile; we usually don't know the answer. So our time was better spent asking, "Now what do we do?" Even with respect to depression, sometimes answering, "Why?" isn't as important as answering, "What do we do about it?" Do you agree with that? Why or why not?

4. Thoughts influence brain chemistry, and brain chemistry influences mood. When you read 2 Corinthians 10:5, how do you now view its importance in light of your mental and physical health?

5. The same enemy who wants to make you feel guilty and condemned for your depression has a very serious character defect highlighted in John 8:44 (NLT): "He has always hated the truth because _____ _____ _____ _____ _____ _____. When he lies, it is consistent with his character; _____ _____ _____ _____ _____ and _____ _____ _____ _____."
If Satan is referred to as the father of lies, why would we believe anything he presents to us?

6. The enemy would like to make you believe that your depression is your fault, but that is yet another lie. Many of the thoughts leading to your depression are not your own thoughts at all, but were planted in your head by the enemy himself, the father of lies. How does that make you feel?

7. While we must battle our thoughts and the lies of the enemy every day, what hope do we find in 1 John 4:4?

8. Hosea 4:6a says, "My people are destroyed from lack of knowledge." To me, that reinforces the importance of knowing what the Word of God says. Did you have the same reaction?

9. We frequently give the enemy permission to influence our lives by the words we say or when we believe his lies. Can you identify times when you have done so? What was the outcome? How did you become aware of it?

10. What promise are we given in James 4:7?

Isn't it comforting to know we have the authority and the ability to close the door and eliminate the influence of the enemy? Practically speaking, what does it look like to "resist the devil" so he will flee?

11. In addition to a spiritual component to depression, chemical, genetic, secondary, and reactionary factors can also contribute.
   • Chemical factors include lower levels of mood-related neurotransmitters (chemicals) in the brain called monoamines.
   • Genetic factors refer to the history of depression in our families that increase the likelihood that we may experience the condition.

- Secondary factors include things like physiology and medical conditions that produce depressive symptoms.
- Reactionary factors include environmental or major life stressors that can contribute to depressive symptoms.

Which, if any, of these factors can you see operating in your situation?

12. A childhood illness with resulting physical deformity opened the door to the spirits of rejection, abandonment, fear, doubt, unbelief, and a poverty mind-set in my life. Additionally, an unloving spirit planted itself in the core of my belief system, making it difficult for me to fully appreciate the Father's unconditional and complete love and impossible to fully love myself or others. I believed the lies of the spirit of perfectionism, self-hatred, self-rejection, self-condemnation, self-pity, self-bitterness, self-resentment, and unforgiveness.
Can you identify the work of any of these at play in your own life?

How have they negatively impacted you?

13. What negative spiritual influence are we warned of in
    2 Timothy 1:7?

What does God supply instead?

The longer I have worked in the field of psychology, the
more convinced I have become that one of the most prevalent ways the enemy influences us is through the spirit of
fear/worry/anxiety. This was certainly true for me. Have
you ever given in to the spirit of fear, and if so, what impact
has it had on your emotional well-being?

14. We cannot rely on our feelings, because they are the out-
    ward manifestation of the thoughts we believe. Is this a
    new concept to you? If so, how does it change your percep-
    tion of your emotions? (If this is not a new concept to you,
    has it impacted how you cope with your emotions?)

15. In the battle against depression, we often must fight against thoughts such as, *I'm always rejected, Nobody loves me, I'll always be this way*, or *I am joy-immune*. Those thoughts are lies from the enemy that, over time, cause us to *feel* depressed. What truths do you know to combat those lies? Write them below. (Need a hint? Try Ephesians 1:6; Jeremiah 31:3; Isaiah 43:19; and Psalm 30:5.)

16. Often, we are unaware of the invisible war waged against us, as well as (sadly) being unaware of what God's truth says about us, which is the very thing that makes us an easy, defenseless target for the enemy. It was true of me. This is true of so many people. Is it true of you, too?

17. Read Isaiah 54:17. What hope does this offer you for every difficult situation?

Key Thoughts ⟿

- While there are chemical, genetic, secondary, and reactionary contributors to depression, we can't ignore the spiritual roots if we truly want healing.
- The spiritual aspect of depression is the reason more individuals aren't effectively treated and/or experience a recurrence.
- We often unknowingly give the enemy permission to influence our lives.
- Our thoughts influence our physical and mental health.
- Most people want to know what caused their depression, but sometimes a better question is, "What do we do about it?"

Your Rx ⟿

Record the following verses on index cards, recite them at least three times daily, and commit them to memory: Psalm 42:5; James 4:7; and Isaiah 54:17.

Recommended Playlist ⟿

"King of the World," Natalie Grant, © 2015 by Curb Records, Inc.
"Press On," Selah, © 2001 by Curb Records, Inc.
"Come As You Are," David Crowder Band © 2014 by sixstepsrecords/Sparrow Records
"Thy Will," Hillary Scott, © 2016 by HST Entertainment/ EMI Records Nashville

Chapter 4

RECOGNIZE THAT YOU HAVE AN ENEMY

"The thief comes only to steal and kill and destroy;
I have come that they may have life,
and have it to the full."
John 10:10

In the dark of night, the security company called to warn that an intruder had entered our premises. I remained calm and fully expected to hear it was a false alarm. When the phone rang a second time to alert me that police were on their way, the potential for harm and loss became very real.

My mind became as thick as cotton, making it difficult to formulate clear thoughts. My hands, clammy from perspiration, failed to hold my drinking glass. My stomach was acutely aware of the boulder that had quickly taken up residence. My feet held frozen to the floor, unable to move as I processed the dispatcher's words.

Being burglarized does something to your sense of safety and security. It opens the memory vault of every time you felt lost, abandoned, rejected, insecure, alone, and afraid. When someone forces themselves into your personal sanctuary and takes what is not theirs, the missing material goods are the least of the fallout. They also steal your peace, kill your joy, and destroy your sense of safety.

From that night, I more self-consciously looked around me as I stood at my door unlocking it, always briefly wondering upon entering what I would find that didn't belong, or what had been taken that was rightfully mine. I remained hyper-vigilant of my surroundings. Who was there as I unlocked my car at the end of the day? Who watched me come and go as I left work? How much could be seen through my windows from outside?

In the time since, I have thought about how easily we hand over our security without any thought. Every day a thief comes in to steal, kill, and destroy from us, and he does so through the access we give him. We hand him the keys to the door of our thoughts and give him free rein. He causes us to think things that are not consistent with what God says in the truth of His Word, thoughts that steal our peace, our joy, and our self-esteem. We must first identify our enemy and then engage our God-given weapons against him.

1. When we are depressed, we need to hold on to hope. What hope-filled promise is given in John 10:10?

2. What is a hope-filled promise from Scripture God has given to you personally?

3. If you have gone through depression or had a friend or loved one who has suffered, how did depression change you/them from your/their non-depressed self?

4. As a doctor who treated depressed patients, when I experienced depression, I felt like a failure. Have you ever felt that way?

   What does God's truth say about this in 2 Corinthians 12:9–10?

5. We have all sinned, yes. But God made a way to look past our sin so that we could stay in good standing with Him. Read 2 Corinthians 5:21 and write it out in your own words here.

6. I have found comfort in the Psalms, but not like most people do. It comforted me to see that the one God called "a man after God's heart" went into and out of and back into the pit of depression. Yet he also offered some of the greatest words of encouragement to those who are in the valley. How do you feel when you read his words of lament such as those in Psalm 109:22: "For I am poor and needy, and my heart is wounded within me"?

7. Jesus looks past the masks we put on for the rest of the world, past the guilt, shame, and despair we feel. He doesn't see our faults or those things we don't like in ourselves. How does that make you feel?

    How do you feel when you realize He sees a wounded child in need of shelter, comfort, and healing?

8. It's always God's desire to comfort His children. Read Isaiah 61:1–3. List the promises God made.

9. When someone is depressed, it's not uncommon for them to believe the lie that they are alone in their suffering and that they are inherently flawed. The enemy produces shame, leaving them feeling alone. Have you ever felt this way, not necessarily even with respect to depression, but perhaps in some other area of your life?

    What truth does God reveal in Romans 8:1?

10. Write out Isaiah 43:2 here. Highlight the wrods "when" in one color, "through" in another color, and "not" in another color.

Three things are evident: (1) God says we will go through difficult times ("when"), (2) we are not going to live in the difficult times forever (we will go "through" them), and (3) the hard times won't do us in ("not"). Does it make you anxious to know you *will* go through these times, or does it bring you more comfort to know they will *not* take you down and that God *will* be with you?

11. We must choose to believe God and trust His promises rather than our feelings. How do we do that when our feelings/emotions are so paramount?

12. For decades, I believed that feelings were neither right nor wrong, they just were. I was deceived because the enemy uses our feelings against us, as if they are truth. I didn't realize that our thoughts influence our feelings. Have you ever been deceived by your feelings? If so, what was the outcome?

What did you learn from it?

13. God promises He won't ever leave us (Deut. 31:6; Heb. 13:5), but He won't force us to stay in His presence either. Have you ever found yourself, like Martha (Luke 10:39–42), being so busy that you missed out on the comfort of being still in His presence?

14. We started off this chapter saying that when we are depressed, we need to hold on to hope. We also reflected on the fact that we must recognize that we have an enemy. Despite the fact that we have an enemy, what hope-filled promise is given in Genesis 50:20?

Key Thoughts ⌒

- We must recognize we have an enemy who wants to make us and keep us depressed.
- Depression turns us into someone we don't recognize.
- Jesus sees us not just as we are, but also as we can be.
- Depression makes us focus on feelings rather than the truth.

Your Rx ⌒

Record the following verses on index cards, recite them at least three times daily, and commit them to memory: John 10:10; Isaiah 43:2; and Genesis 50:20.

Recommended Playlist ⁓

"I Am Not Alone," Kari Jobe, © 2014 by Sparrow Records

"Enough," Natalie Grant, © 2015 by Curb Records, Inc.

"From the Inside Out," Hillsong United, © 2010 by Hillsong Church T/A Hillsong Music Australia

"Unfinished," Mandisa, © 2017 by Sparrow Records

Chapter 5

RECOVER YOUR JOY

Those who sow with tears will reap with songs of joy.
Psalm 126:5

There were days, weeks, months even, when I wondered if the darkness would ever lift, if depression would ever become a distant memory. Laughter had become a thing of the past; why couldn't depression?

The valley of depression was the journey I traveled, and I had begun to wonder if I was just joy-immune. Perhaps you've wondered that too. But friend, that is a lie from the enemy of our souls—a lie set up to steal our joy, kill our peace, and destroy our identity. The truth is, we are more than overcomers. We are victorious in Christ Jesus. The Word says that God is doing a *new* thing in us!

One of the ways the enemy keeps us in the depths of the valley of depression is by stealing our joy. He does that largely through our thoughts. One way to combat that is to take captive every thought, which means to consciously think about the thoughts we have and determine whether they line up with God's Word.

Depression is hard. When you're in the midst of it, it feels unending. But it will end. If you listen to God's Word, follow His principles, and hold on to His hand, it will end. I'm living proof.

God promises in His Word that weeping may last for a night, but just like the sunrise, joy comes in the morning.

1. The enemy attempts to bring on depression by stealing our joy. What hope-filled promise is given in Psalm 126:5?

2. One of the enemy's primary tactics as it relates to depression is to steal our joy, and this diminishes our enthusiasm for all things. In doing so, he takes that which attracts others to us and thus to God. People are attracted to those filled with joy, so in stealing our joy, we are less attractive to others. Yet God's Word *commands* us to consider it an opportunity for joy when troubles come (James 1:2). How do you reconcile that?

3. When you're in the midst of a difficult trial, depression or
    otherwise, it can be hard to "be glad that you are in the very
    thick of what Christ experienced" (1 Peter 4:12–13). What
    is the promise that we must cling to in verse 13?

    It can be hard to hold on to gladness and hope in the midst
    of depression. But what is the promise we have 1 Peter 4
    and now in Isaiah 57:15?

4. Desperation made me willing to search for God's answers
    as I walked through my darkest days. It made me seek
    harder, pray more fervently, and surrender everything. Has
    desperation ever made you willing to do something? To
    learn something? To listen to God? To obey God? How has
    desperation had a positive impact on your life?

5.   Many have the notion that we can just manufacture joy, but
     Scripture suggests that it is *a gift from God* (John 15:10–12;
     Rom. 15:13). That truth took much of the pressure off me.
     Yet it also indicates that some of the responsibility lies with
     us, because it says we must trust God, recover ourselves,
     recognize we have cooperated with the enemy and agreed
     with his lies, repent to God and, if necessary, to others, re-
     nounce and reject the enemy's lies, and receive God's love,
     forgiveness, peace, and joy. That's a lot of work. What part
     of this equation do you find the hardest and why?

6.   If joy is a gift, then to have true joy, we must have an ac-
     curate perspective of *the Giver of all joy*, yet many of us do
     not. What characteristics of God do the following verses
     highlight?
     Psalm 86:15: _____ _____

     _____ _____

     Job 19:25   _____
     Romans 8:32   _____
     Ephesians 1:7–8   _____ _____

     _____

7.   According to Romans 15:13, what must we do before God
     will fill us with His joy and peace?

8. What did David declare in Psalm 16:11 and Psalm 21:6 as our first defense when we desire to recover our joy?

Yet so often, that's the last thing people are inclined to do when they are depressed. They don't want to be with anyone—including God. But if it is true that "healing and restoration come when we get so close and personal with Jesus that no one can come between us,"[3] how do we combat the tendency to withdraw when we are depressed?

9. Write Out Psalm 68:3 here.

This verse suggests that we must first choose to be glad and rejoice, and then we will experience happiness and joy. At first glance, that seems counterintuitive. How do you reconcile that?

10. Read Mark 11:24 and 1 John 5:14–15. Consciously praising God and determining to thank Him in advance for His answers was part of my joy-producing perspective rather than a joy-defeating perspective. What other joy-producing and joy-defeating qualities and behaviors can you identify from your own experience?

11. Look up John 16:24 and Romans 12:12. What is a common contributor to maintaining our joy in both Scriptures?

12. It is difficult to remain depressed and truly grateful at the same time. Would you agree with this statement? Why or why not?

13. In the Psalms, David repeatedly refers to the importance of gratitude despite our trials. In Psalm 50:14 and Psalm 116:17, he specifically spoke of "sacrificing a thank offering." The word *sacrifice* suggests it isn't easy. *Offering* indicates it's a gift. *Thanks* suggests that it is given out of gratitude. What would sacrificing a thank offering look like when you are dealing with depression?

14. It's been said that comparison is the thief of joy. Whenever I start comparing myself to others and their accomplishments, it's a slippery slope, leading to feeling down about myself. In our current culture, comparison is rampant. When we read Philippians 4:11 and 1 Thessalonians 5:18, how can we reconcile comparison with gratitude? And how do they impact our emotional functioning?

15. Proverbs 23:7 says we are what we think in our hearts. How does that impact your motivation to guard both your heart and your thought life?

Key Thoughts ⟋

- The enemy attempts to steal our joy.
- Desperation makes us willing—let's make sure it's for the right thing.
- Joy is a gift from God.
- A fast track to losing our joy is focusing on ourselves instead of on God.

Your Rx ⟋

Record the following verses on index cards, recite them at least three times daily, and commit them to memory: Psalm 126:5; Romans 15:13; Psalm 68:3; and Romans 12:12.

Recommended Playlist ⟋

"O Praise Him (All This for a King)," David Crowder Band, © 2003 Sparrow Records/sixstepsrecords

"Ever Be," Bethel Music & Kalley Heiligenthal, © 2015 by Bethel Music

"Where Joy and Sorrow Meet," Avalon, © 2006 by Sparrow Records

"The Comeback," Danny Gokey, © 2017 by BMG Rights Management (US) LLC

Chapter 6

RECLAIM YOUR PEACE

Now may the Lord of peace himself give you peace at all times
and in every way. The Lord be with all of you.
2 Thessalonians 3:16

We didn't ask for it, and we weren't prepared for it when
it struck. In fact, the most devastating news came at what was
supposed to be our most joyous occasion in years. The doctor's confirmation that my husband had cancer came the same
day *Hope Prevails* released. The launch party and major book
signing event were planned within a few days, yet amidst the
celebrating, our hearts were breaking.

We had walked this path before—a different form, but
cancer nonetheless. We weren't newbies. We had visions from
the previous experience infiltrating our minds. The treatment
would be similar—unwelcome but necessary.

The truth is, cancer stinks. Cancer hurts. Cancer doesn't just affect the one diagnosed; it impacts the entire family and to some degree, friends and extended family as well. Nobody asks for it, and nobody wants to go through it—much like depression.

Cancer and depression are our enemies, and just like the enemy of our souls, they seek to steal, kill, and destroy. If that is what we focus on, that is what will happen. But as with everything in life, it's a matter of perspective, and we get to choose our perspective.

Indeed, we will all go through difficult times, the cancerous times: relationship difficulty, financial strains, health issues, job problems, etc. They aren't wanted or invited. But the even greater truth is that we don't walk through these trials alone, and Jesus promised in John 16:33 that we can have peace through them. So while the fiery darts are flying and we are walking through this valley, we do so with swords drawn, prayers raised, and our faith strong in the One who has already overcome it all and offers His peace through it.

⌒

1. The enemy attempts to bring on depression by killing our peace. What hope-filled promise are we given in 2 Thessalonians 3:16?

2. How would you characterize peace?

3. What is the name of God given in Judges 6:24?

4. Read John 14:27 and John 16:33. These two verses indicate
    that peace comes from where? _____
    As a what? _____

    The key is that *in Him* we can have peace, not on our own.
    In what ways do you find yourself sacrificing your peace?

5. One of the quickest ways the enemy can get us to surrender
    our peace is to cause us to become anxious. When we are
    anxious, we are not at peace. Anxiety results from feeling
    out of control. But if we surrender to God, letting Him
    be in control, we can remain in perfect peace. Which four
    keys does Paul give us to maintain our peace in Philippians
    4:6–7?

    _____
    _____
    _____
    _____

6. When we worry, we believe the enemy's lies, taking our eyes off of God and focusing on ourselves and our circumstances. Why do you think it's so easy to worry and sometimes so hard to trust God?

   Read Matthew 6:25; 6:30–33; and 1 Peter 5:7. What motivation are we given not to worry?

7. Fear is a waste of our energy and robs us of peace. It causes us to focus on our own abilities rather than on God and His solutions. To reclaim your peace, what can you do to keep your focus on the Solver of your problems rather than on your circumstances? Proverbs 3:5–6 gives some wise counsel. Write it out here.

   ~ When we replace worry with prayer, we trust. ~

8. Turn back to Luke 10:39–42. Why, oh why, do we compare our deficiencies to others' strengths, our lack to others' plenty, and our pain to others' joy, especially when the focus on the negative only serves to obstruct our view and kill our peace? This is exactly what Martha did, and it made her miserable.

It seems that if we even thought about it briefly, we would realize it doesn't serve us very well.

9. We must deliberately choose a right attitude. What does Philippians 4:8 tell us to think about?

For reflection: Do you ever struggle with this? How do you do this when your feelings are such powerful dictators?

10. Philippians 4:8 is a well-known verse about thinking positively, but it also means we are to think positively about ourselves. How much more difficult is it for you to apply this verse to yourself? Why?

11. The Holy Spirit convicts us of our mistakes to bring about change, but the enemy shames us to makes us think we *are* our mistakes. How does the enemy use shame to interfere in your life and kill your peace?

What is the truth God says about you in:

Romans 8:1:

Ephesians 1:9; Colossians 1:13–14; and 1 John 2:12:

Ephesians 4:24 and 2 Corinthians 5:21:

Isaiah 43:1:

1 Corinthians 15:57:

For reflection: Those are words of power and victory, so why are you listening to a liar and a defeatist?

12. "We lose our peace when we hide our brokenness."[4] Has
    there ever been a time when shame over something in your
    life made you keep something hidden in the dark, but
    when it finally came out into the light, you experienced
    relief?

    What does 1 John 1:7 have to say about that?

13. The stigma that surrounds mental health issues like depres-
    sion saddens me. Maybe it would help to look at some of
    the biblical greats who also struggled. Who can you iden-
    tify in the following passages?
    Numbers 11:10–15: _____
    Ruth 1:13, 20–21: _____
    1 Samuel 1:7–10: _____
    1 Samuel 16:14–23: _____
    1 Samuel 30:4–6: _____
    1 Kings 19:4–5: _____
    Job 30:16–26: _____
    Jonah 4:1–9: _____
    2 Corinthians 1:8–10: _____
    Matthew 26:38; Luke 22:41, 44; John 11:35: _____

    According to Isaiah 26:3, what is the secret to keeping our
    peace?

And by extension, how about in Philippians 4:13?

14. Bitterness and unforgiveness in our hearts prevent us from
    being at peace. Hebrews 12:15 goes so far as to say it causes
    us _____. Is there someone you need to for-
    give today? If we desire God's peace, we must live peaceably
    with others by forgiving others. Have you ever experienced
    a return or an infilling of peace after extending forgiveness
    to someone?

15. God has already forgiven you (Ps. 103:8–12; Acts 10:42–
    43; and Col. 1:13–14). When we talk about forgiveness,
    we forget that the person we sometimes most need to for-
    give is ourselves. Write out Hebrews 9:14 here.

When we don't forgive ourselves, we deny the work of the
cross and trivialize the sacrifice of Jesus' life for our sins.
He already paid the price and did so with great joy. Nothing can undo that sacrifice. Now it's time to appreciate it.
Don't let the enemy hold you hostage in unforgiveness to-
ward yourself any longer! Prayerfully search your heart. Is
there anything you need to forgive yourself for?

16. In the valley of depression, the spirit of self-pity often tempts us to feel like we are void of choices, a victim of the circumstances and reactions of those around us. But the truth is that Scripture clearly says as a man "thinketh in his heart, so is he" (Prov. 23:7a KJV). What are we told to do in 2 Corinthians 10:5 as our best defense?

Clearly, if God tells us to take every thought captive, He will give us the ability to do so. Have you ever fallen prey to the temptation to believe you didn't have a choice in how to respond in a situation? I've been tempted to believe that, but then in His love and mercy, God whispered His truth to my heart. I not only have a choice, but He gives me the ability to take those thoughts captive. How does the truth of these two Scriptures change your perception that you don't have a choice?

17. Our Savior died so we could have better than a life of depression and the fullest possible joy. What is the promise made in the second half of John 10:10?

Do you believe that for yourself?

Key Thoughts ⌒

- The enemy's mission is to kill our peace.
- Anxiety is the absence of peace; worry comes from believing the enemy's lies.
- We lose our peace by focusing on ourselves and our problems.
- We reclaim our peace by focusing on and trusting God, the Solver of our problems.

Your Rx ⌒

Record the following verses on index cards, recite them at least three times daily, and commit them to memory: John 16:33; Philippians 4:6–7; and Isaiah 26:3.

Recommended Playlist ⌒

"Breathe," Rebecca St. James, © 2002 by ForeFront Records

"Forever," Kari Jobe, © 2014 by Sparrow Records

"We Will Not Be Shaken," Bethel Music, © 2015 by Bethel Music

"Even If," MercyMe, © 2017 by MercyMe

Chapter 7

REESTABLISH YOUR IDENTITY

You, dear children, are from God and have overcome them,
because the one who is in you is greater than the one who
is in the world.
1 John 4:4

I sat with my back pinned against the back of the upright chair, legs crossed, assessing my choice of attire for the evening from the boots to the pants to the lace blouse, and finished off with the jewelry—never leave home without it. Was my choice appropriate for the evening? It seemed to blend in sufficiently with Executive Ellen's and Powerhouse Pam's attire. I didn't mean to, but I was in comparison mode. Oh, how I hated that—I always ended up on the short end of the stick.

I spent the evening planning an upcoming event with other area ministry leaders, honored to be included but secretly wondering how I had made the guest list. These were high-powered women with years of impressive, successful ministry behind them. They each knew their call and they had confidently lived and breathed it each day for decades. As I sat listening to their suggestions, I fought to ignore another deafening voice—one that sought to mock me at every turn.

"Why are you even here? You don't belong here. You're not as important as they are. What have you done for the kingdom of God that even comes close to comparing with these women?"

The evening left me feeling useless. Minimized. Devalued. Unworthy.

I'm not sure how I saw through my tears to drive home that night, but by the time I arrived in my garage, I turned off the ignition, sat in the solitude of my parked car, and wept. The possibility that I wasn't making an impact for God grieved my heart.

A friend later asked about my evening, then encouraged me to pray and ask God what He thought. I admitted my fear of His answer, to which she lovingly reminded me, "It's not His nature or character to criticize you. He only encourages, exhorts, and builds you up."

As I sought the Lord for answers, it was as if He whispered to my heart, *"The enemy likes to tell you who you* aren't *and always in the* negative, *but I delight in telling you who you are and always in the* positive."

Tears flowed as I let those words seep into my heart. I had listened to the negative lies of the enemy: *You're useless. You're not trustworthy. God doesn't value you as much as others. Your purpose isn't as important.*

Let's stop playing the enemy's comparison game and start living in our Christ-bought identity. There is eternal security there.

1. The enemy attempts to bring on depression by destroying our identity. What is the hope-filled promise given in 1 John 4:4?

   What are your first thoughts when you read that Scripture?

2. Sometimes it only takes one simple word for the enemy to mess with our minds and cause us to doubt. He's been doing it since his entrance in the garden. Turn to Genesis 3:1. What was the one word that caused Eve to question what she knew to be true?

   List examples of when he whispered the same word to you, which ultimately made you doubt your identity (e.g., Do you *really* think you are as smart as them? You don't *really* think they would accept you if they knew about your past, do you?)

3. "If we do not remain vigilant about identifying which voices we listen to and hence believe, we will unconsciously exchange our beliefs about our identity for convincing counterfeits."[5]

   In Luke 1:26–38, Mary believed she had heard a message from the Lord, surrendered herself to His will, and had glorious eternal consequences when she gave birth to the Messiah. In a quite different scenario, we can read the account of Judas listening to the influence of the spirits of pride and greed when he betrayed Jesus for thirty pieces of silver in Luke 22:47–48. Feeling such guilt for his deed and listening to counterfeit voices had devastating consequences for Judas, as we read of his suicide in Matthew 27:1–5.

   For reflection: What convincing counterfeits have you believed in the past?

4. If you did as Brennan Manning suggested and "defined yourself radically as one beloved by God,"[6] and every other identity was just an illusion, how would your day-to-day life be different?

How would your personality be different?

How would your relationships be different?

5. Have you ever thought about the fact that God gave us the ultimate compliment when He created us in His perfect image?

What else did He say about us in the following passages:

Psalm 139:14:

Ephesians 2:10:

Did you ever consider that when God looked at us, His masterpiece, He declared us "good"?

6. Look up the following Scriptures and write them out here:

Ephesians 1:6:

1 Corinthians 3:23:

1 John 4:4:

Each of these verses emphasize equating our identity with _____.

The problem comes when we are more apt to believe what others say, and then we say those same things about ourselves.

For reflection: When have you fallen prey to believing what others have said about you instead of what God has said?

What needs to change for you to come into agreement with what God says?

7. I learned through a life-threatening illness, when I was unable to *do* anything, that God isn't looking for perfection or even productivity. He just wants a relationship.
The truth is, you are more than:
your personality,
your talents,
your career,
your bank account,
your relationships,
your past,
your successes, or
your failures.

According to John 1:12, the greatest thing about you is that you are:

For reflection: Have you ever fallen prey to the lie that you had to do more or be perfect in order for God to love you? How did you break free from that lie (or have you)?

8. What do James 3:9–10 and Proverbs 18:21 say about the influence of our words?

So often we allow our identity to be shaped by the opinions of others, or the blessings or curses spoken over us, rather than the truth of what God says.

For reflection: How has your identity been adversely impacted by listening to the influence of anyone other than God?

9. The enemy first likes to point out our faults and all we are not, but he then likes to persuade us to hide, to shrink back, and to avoid stepping up and stepping out to be all God created us to be. He does this by getting us to focus our attention on our faults, on our lack, rather than on who God is and who He says we are. Let's return to the truth of what God says:

When God _____ you, He said it was _____. (Gen. 1:31)

God has a _____ for you, and it is _____. (Jer. 29:11)

God began a _____ work in you, and He is going to finish it! (Phil. 1:6)

God is incapable of anything other than good, and the common theme here is that in His eyes, *you are* _____.

10. Have you ever fallen prey to comparison? Where or how does it affect you the most?

What do Ephesians 1:7 and Colossians 1:14 say that God did for us?

The price paid for an item determines its value. Christ paid the same price for each of us when He gave up His life and died for each of us on the cross. That levels the playing field, so there's no need for us to compare ourselves to each other.

11. Self-hatred is one of the most problematic issues in terms of embracing our identity in Christ. That might seem a little harsh, but if you think about it, we cannot agree with two kingdoms at once. If we do not agree with what God says about us (and He *loves* us completely), then we can quickly fall into self-hatred when the enemy offers up our faults for inspection and we agree with him, especially when he tempts us to compare ourselves to others.

For reflection: What have you decided you are less of when you compare yourself to others?

12. Have you ever struggled to receive God's forgiveness because the enemy convinced you that your flaws were too big? That's another lie of the enemy.

Isaiah 53:6 says, "We _____, like sheep, have gone astray, _____ ___ ____ has turned to our own way; and the Lord has laid on him the iniquity of us _____."

Except for Jesus, who was perfect in every way, what does Romans 3:23 say?

And what assurance does Colossians 2:13 give us?

We have *all* sinned, yet Christ died for the forgiveness of *all* sins. The enemy is a liar.

13. Have you ever given up your dreams or the longings of your heart because of another's opinions or lies from the enemy?

What encouragement do Jeremiah 29:11 and Philippians 1:6 give you?

14. Every day the enemy whispers (or shouts!) lies at you to destroy your identity and make you depressed. The best way to combat the enemy is with the truth of God's Word. For many years, I didn't know what God said about me. Do you? Find out here and commit these verses to memory.

    You are _____. (Ps. 45:11)

    You are _____. (Rom. 8:37)

    You are _____ forever. (Jer. 31:3)

    You are _____ _____. (John 15:15)

    You are _____ _____ _____. (Eph. 2:6)

    You are the _____. (Zech. 2:8)

    You are _____ and _____ _____. (Col. 3:12)

    You are _____. (Matt. 6:26)

    He _____ you. (Ps. 103:12)

    He persistently _____ you. (Luke 19:10)

Key Thoughts ⌒

- The enemy desires to destroy our identity.
- When God made us, He declared it to be good; it's the enemy who points out and magnifies our faults.
- God loves us not because of what we do but because of whose we are.
- Reestablish your identity by declaring over yourself the good things God says about you.

Your Rx ⟿

Record the following verses on index cards, recite them at least three times daily, and commit them to memory: 1 John 4:4; John 1:12; and Proverbs 18:21.

Recommended Playlist ⟿

"Unusual," Francesca Battistelli, © 2014 by Word Entertainment LLC

"Dear Younger Me," MercyMe, © 2014 by Fair Trade/Columbia

"Good Father," Chris Tomlin, © 2015 by sixstepsrecords/Sparrow Records

"You Never Let Go," Matt Redman, © 2006 by sixstepsrecords/Sparrow Records

Chapter 8

KNOW YOUR WORTH

But now, this is what the LORD says . . . "Do not fear, for I
have redeemed you;
I have summoned you by name; you are mine."
Isaiah 43:1

I'll never forget the day my young son came home from
school despondent, lacking his normal carefree smile. When I
scooped him up in a hug and attempted to lighten the mood
with a tickle-fest, I was instead greeted with tears. "Mom, some
kids at school said I wasn't smart enough to sit at the cool kids'
table."

I thought my heart was going to shatter in front of this
sweet boy who had a heart of gold and the most generous spirit
to boot. I could tell him it wasn't true. I could tell him what I
thought. More importantly, I would share with him what God
said because He's the only One whose opinion counts.

I spent many years listening to wrong opinions and the enemy's lies about my identity, too many years, in fact, not really appreciating what God said about me. I lived too long believing God was mad at me, and that He needed me to be perfect in order to love me.

I grew up in the Church and attended every time the doors were open. I even won my share of Bible verse drills in Sunday school. Yet if I'm being honest with you, something was missing: I didn't really know what God said about me. That made me easy prey for the enemy of my soul to flood my mind and my heart with lies that stole my joy, killed my peace, and destroyed my identity.

What I didn't know then was exactly what my son needed to know to settle the issue of his worth and to realize that while others may reject us, we are accepted by the only One whose opinion counts.

1. What is the hope-filled promise in Isaiah 43:1?

2. Brené Brown said, "What we know matters, but who we are matters more."[7] When you take that into account with the affirmation in Isaiah 43:1b, what does that do for your sense of self-worth?

3. What are we repeatedly told in Scripture about God's love?
   Hosea 14:4: "I will love them _____."
   Romans 8:32 (KJV): He "shall _____
   _____ us all things."
   Ephesians 1:6" "which he has _____ _____
   us in the One he loves."

Newborn babies do nothing to earn their parents' *free gift*
of love; all they must do is receive it. So why then do we so
easily get caught up in trying to earn God's love at the very
least, struggle to receive it, when He *freely gives* it?

4. The temptation today is to equate our worth with external
   factors, or to be influenced by the words, attitudes, or ac-
   tions of others. Were you ever the recipient of another's
   words that either positively or negatively shaped what you
   believed to be true about yourself?

Anything anyone else (including the enemy) has ever said
about you cannot compare to what God has done and said
about you.

He _____ you. (Eph. 1:5)
He _____ you. (Isa. 43:1)
He _____ you His. (Ps. 95:7; Ps. 100:3;
Isa. 43:1)

5. According to John 15:13, what is the greatest expression of love one could give?

Matthew 20:28 reveals, "just as the Son of man did not come to be served, but to serve, and to _____ _____ _____ as a ransom for many."

John 3:16 reminds us that, "For God so loved the world that he gave his one and only Son, that _____ believes in him shall not perish but have eternal life."

"Whoever" is *you!* Consider now just how valuable you are because of the greatest expression of love and the highest price paid for you with the cost of Christ's death on the cross. Jesus is the only One who has paid the price of His life for you—He is the only One who has any authority to declare your worth!

We have a very real enemy, and our fear of him only enhances his power. He would like us to believe that we are slaves to our past, to our mistakes, to our sin, even to our depression. But *every fear is based on a lie.*

6. What promise-filled truth are we given in John 8:36?

Our sin and shame were replaced with Christ's perfection, our death replaced by His life, and our bondage replaced by His freedom when He died on the cross and declared that the work was finished.

For reflection: What keeps you from living in that freedom and kicking the enemy to the curb?

7. We all like money, or at least what it allows us to do. If I offered you a crisp, clean $100 bill, you'd likely take it. If I crumpled it up in my hand first, you'd still willingly receive it. If I tossed it on the ground and even stepped on it, you'd still probably pick it up. Why? Because none of those experiences changed the value of that bill.

What promise are we given in Genesis 50:20a?

What promise are we given in Romans 8:28?

Just like the tattered and blemished $100 bill, do you ever find yourself feeling less acceptable because of the blemishes life has brought your way? That's when we must hold on to the promises in Genesis 50:20 and Romans 8:28.

8. In a depressed state, one of the last things we might *feel* is
    treasured, valued, or accepted. That's when we must make
    the conscious choice to believe the truth of God's Word
    over our feelings. What does God's truth say about you in
    the following verses?

Isaiah 49:16:

Isaiah 62:3:

Song of Solomon 4:9:

Ephesians 1:5–7:

For reflection: What makes you forget or doubt your worth
the most?

Consider placing a dot in the center of your palm with a
pen every day for a week. Every time you see it, let it be a
visual reminder that you are so worthy that Christ took
nails in His palms for you.

Key Thoughts ⌒

- We are accepted by the only One whose opinion counts.
- God calls us His—we are sons and daughters of the Most High God.
- We have infinite worth because Christ gave His life to save us.
- When we focus on how much God loves us and the cost He endured to redeem us, then we can appreciate our worth.

Your Rx ⌒

Record the following verses on index cards, recite them at least three times daily, and commit them to memory: Isaiah 43:1; John 8:36; and Isaiah 49:16.

Recommended Playlist ⌒

"All I Need," Gateway Worship, © 2010 by Integrity/Columbia
"No Longer Slaves," Bethel Music, © 2015 by Bethel Music
"Mended," Matthew West, © 2015 by Sparrow Records
"I Won't Let You Go," Switchfoot, © 2016 by Vanguard Records

Chapter 9

REMEMBER YOUR SECURE DESTINY

"My Father, who has given them to me, is greater than all;
no one can snatch them out of my Father's hand."
John 10:29

During my journey through the valley of depression, God showed me that if we want joy, we must trust Him. Sometimes, however, I get wrapped up in "the doing" for God. I want to please Him by what I do and attempt to prove myself worthy by trying to be perfect. But that's not what pleases Him. What makes God happy is when we trust. In fact, He says that without faith (trust), it is impossible to please Him (Heb. 11:6). Despite all the times David wallowed in his misery in the Psalms, he continually came back to, "and yet I will trust Him"! That's what pleased God.

During difficult trials, my trust muscle often seems weak. I find it hard to trust myself because my feelings are unpredictable and simply the outward manifestation of the thoughts I've believed. I struggle to trust others because their words often relay a lack of understanding or compassion. Embarrassingly, I often also struggle to trust God, even though that's my heart's desire.

Repeatedly, I prayed for God to help me trust Him more. One morning as I prayed the same prayer again, I sensed God saying, "*We've been over this before.*"

We had—numerous days in a row. "Yes, Lord, I know. I just keep struggling. Please help me to trust You more."

He surprised me with His response, "It's really not that complicated. It's your choice. Either you choose to trust Me, or you don't. Either you believe in Me, or you don't. Either you believe I'm sovereign, or you don't. Don't make it any more difficult than that."

It's a choice. It's a risk. But what did I have to lose? My control? My responsibility? My burden? My worry? Wasn't that worth the risk?

God isn't looking for our perfect efforts. It's because of our imperfection that He sent Jesus. And because of Jesus, our destiny is secure. We don't have to work for it. He just wants us to trust Him, despite what we see in our circumstances.

1. When we are depressed, the enemy will even have us questioning our destiny. What is the hope-filled promise in John 10:29?

2. Society often readily buys in to the enemy's lie that our past predicts our future. But the truth is that God determines our future and His Word declares that "no one can snatch them out of my Father's hand" (John 10:29). What's your reaction to that? How does that belief become apparent in your life?

3. I'm so grateful that God gives us examples in the Bible of those who have gone before us and struggled with the same issues we do today. I've had a temper tantrum or two with God when I was hurt, frustrated, and wanted Him to act more quickly. Read the accounts of Jonah's and Job's "tantrums" in Jonah 4:1–2 and Job 7:11–21. In my own experience and in theirs, God was so invested in the relationship that He was willing to deal with the tantrum, and because He cares about our relationship with Him, He doesn't let those tantrums, our past, or our depression ruin our secure destiny.

For reflection: Have you ever had a temper tantrum with God and been so vulnerable that you told Him of your anger and hurt? How did He respond? What did you learn in that exchange?

4. Several influences worked together to keep me firmly entrenched in depression's valley: self-pity, self-doubt, self-accusation, rejection, fear of failure, fear of abandonment, drivenness, and perfectionism. We can find many of these operating in the lives of those in the Bible. Match up the individual on the left with an area of negative influence in their life on the right.

    1. __ Moses (Exodus 4:1–13)   a. Self-pity
    2. __ David (Psalm 13:1–6)   b. Inferiority
    3. __ Naomi (Ruth 1:20–21)   c. Fear of failure
    4. __ Zacchaeus (Luke 19:1–7)   d. Self-doubt
    5. __ Martha (Luke 10:38–42)   e. Abandonment
    6. __ The Hebrew people   f. Drivenness
          (Numbers 13:26–31)

For reflection: Can you see any of these at work in your own life? How have they served you?

5. Much of my life was spent unconsciously striving to be good enough. What is the hope-filled promise given in Romans 3:24?

And in 1 Corinthians 1:30?

Do you ever find yourself striving to be a good enough parent? Spouse? Friend? Church member? Volunteer? Employee? The truth is that because of Christ's sacrifice, we are declared *enough*.

For reflection: Can you look in the mirror today and remind yourself that because of Christ, you *are* enough?

6. In the valley of our trials, it's hard to see past our pain to the joyful future God has for us, or to believe that God won't leave us in the painful valley. In Isaiah 61, God promises that our destiny includes the following:

v. 1: "He has sent me to _____ _____
the brokenhearted, to proclaim _____
for the captives and _____ from darkness for the prisoners."

v. 2: "To _____ all who mourn."

v. 3: "To bestow on them a _____ of _____ instead of ashes, the _____ of _____ instead of mourning, and a _____ of _____ instead of despair."

v. 6: "You will be called _____ of the LORD, you will be named _____ of our God. You will feed on the _____ of nations, and in their riches, you will boast."

v. 7: "Instead of your shame you will receive a _____ _____, and instead of disgrace you will rejoice in your _____. And so you will inherit a _____ _____ in your landz and _____ _____ will be yours."

For reflection: What keeps you from believing those promises for your destiny?

7. When I was at my weakest, both physically and emotionally, I was tempted to admit defeat. Determining to win the war against the enemy of my soul took *work,* and there were times when I wondered if the fight was worth the effort. (And he counted on that!) I had to stand on the hope-filled promises of the verses below. What are the promises found in each?

Romans 8:37:

Philippians 4:13:

1 Corinthians 15:57:

2 Corinthians 2:14:

Have you ever been there, ready to give up? What kept you going?

How will these promises help you in the future?

8. One way the enemy attacks is by getting us to worry about our future, ours or our children's—something none of us can control. Do you ever fall prey to the enemy's temptation to worry about your future? How do you respond? How well does that serve you?

To combat it, we must first recognize where it comes from:

2 Timothy 1:7a (KJV): "For _____ hath not given us the _____ of fear."

Remember, Ephesians 6:12 (KJV) reminds us, "For we wrestle not against _____ and _____, but against _____, against _____, against the _____ of the _____ of this world, against _____ _____ in high places."

Worry and fear come from the same enemy, discussed in John 10:10. To combat worry and fear, we must stand on the truth-filled promise declared in 2 Timothy 1:7b.

9. Both faith and fear carry equal weight and both demand our focus, yet you get to choose which will reign. Choosing faith over fear or doubt will have profoundly positive results. Consider the encouragement given in Hebrews 11:11.

Refresh your memory of the story of the father and his son who was ill from an evil spirit in Mark 9:14–29. When the father vacillated between faith and doubt, what does verse 24 tell us he did?

10. What example does that provide us with for the times when we struggle to choose between faith and fear?

Sometimes fear traps are so subtle we don't even recognize them for what they are, and we just accept them and ride the wave. Unfortunately, fear, worry, and anxiety often start small, and if we don't deal with them appropriately, they build and become almost insurmountable. I've learned that when I think, *What if. . .?* I'm stepping into a fear/anxiety trap set by the enemy of my soul. What does Matthew 6:27 tell us about the futility of worrying?

What does 1 Peter 5:7 say we should do when we are worried?

For reflection: What are some of the traps the enemy sets for you that take you into fear or anxiety?

11. Every day, every hour, every minute, the enemy whispers thoughts into our minds, hoping we will come into agreement with his lies. But God gives us His truth and the prompting of His Holy Spirit to help us course-correct. What hope-filled promise is given in 1 Corinthians 10:13?

For reflection: How well do you do with course-correcting the negative internal dialogue in your mind about yourself or others? How might you do this differently?

Key Thoughts

- Your past does not predict your future—God does.
- God accepts us despite our imperfections and declares that we are enough.
- Both fear and faith demand our focus, but we can trust God despite our circumstances.
- Because of Christ's finished work on the cross, our destiny is secured.

Your Rx

Record the following verses on index cards, recite them at least three times daily, and commit them to memory: John 10:29; Romans 8:37; 2 Timothy 1:7; Matthew 6:27; and 1 Peter 5:7.

Recommended Playlist

"Stronger," Mandisa, © 2011 by Sparrow Records

"Beautiful One," Jeremy Camp, © 2004 by Brandon Ebel Company

"Just Say Jesus," 7eventh Time Down, © 2013 by BEC Recordings

"Lord, I'm Ready Now," Plumb © 2012 by Curb Records

Chapter 10

BE CONFIDENT THAT NOTHING SEPARATES YOU FROM GOD'S LOVE

So that Christ may dwell in your hearts through faith.
And I pray that you, being rooted and established in love,
may have power together with all the Lord's holy people, to
grasp how wide and long and high and deep is the
love of Christ.
Ephesians 3:17–18

Because an illness shortly after my third birthday left me with a deformed leg and foot, I spent forty years in pain and struggling to find shoes to fit. My normal foot was an average woman's size, but the deformed foot struggled to awkwardly fit a shoe half that size from the little girl's department. And shoe designers just didn't make matching shoes to span both sizes, so fitting both feet at the same time was a challenge.

Over the years, the deformity worsened and the daily pain became more than I could take, prompting yet another reconstructive foot surgery. Just one more thing in a list so long I had lost count. My hopes were high this time for a new foot. A beautiful foot. A normal foot.

I counted down the weeks and days until I would finally be able to wear a beautiful pair of shoes like all my friends. I had the pair ready, displayed in my closet for the big reveal. When the surgeon allowed me to ditch the surgical boot and begin wearing regular shoes, I excitedly pulled out the beautiful pair I had purchased in anticipation of the occasion.

Except they didn't fit. Not only did that pair not fit my new foot, but not a single shoe in my closet fit either. My only option was the big, ugly, black surgical boot. This served as a daily reminder of my flaws and inadequacies.

Not one to ever really express my anger to God (after all, I had read the book of Job—I knew how God responded to Job when he asked, "Why?"), I had never felt safe expressing my hurt and anger for my disfigurement to God. Until that day—the day I had a temper tantrum with God. That day I cried years' worth of tears in despair and frustration. That day I finally got honest and unburdened my heart and told God how I really felt.

I chuckled through my tears as I "heard" Him say, *"At least you're talking to Me about it now."*

You see, I had believed the enemy's lies when he whispered into my ear, *"Don't tell God how you really feel—He'll get angry, stop loving you, and leave you."*

As my sobs slowed to a stream of tears flowing down my cheeks, an image was seared in my heart of Cinderella as she lost her shoe running from the palace at midnight. What was that supposed to mean? Was that some kind of cruel joke?

Seeking God about this image, I sensed Him saying, "*You are not your deformity. What I see is your heart, which is beautiful. I created you in My image—to Me you will always be beautiful.*" In the Cinderella fairy tale, the prince searched high and low for her, not despite her lost shoe, but because of it. In the same way, God searched for me, loving me perfectly in my imperfection, all the while I had tried to hide it. I may never be perfect (or have beautiful, normal feet), but that's why Jesus came to die for me. He loved me (and you) so much, He thought we were worth dying for!

1. What is the hope-filled promise of Ephesians 3:17–18?

2. Do you ever wear a mask not showing the real you out of fear that people wouldn't love or accept you if they knew all your faults and mistakes? It's such a comfort that we don't have to wear a mask with God—He loves us just the way we are. What are the hope-filled promises He gives in Romans 5:8 and Ephesians 2:4–5 for why we can discard the masks?

    Romans 5:8:

    Ephesians 2:4–5:

3. The enemy wants to convince us that because we *feel* alone,
   we *are* alone. In depression's valley, we tend to focus inward
   on ourselves and how we feel, rather than on others or on
   God, which allows the enemy's voice to get louder. What
   truth is offered in the following promises?

   Genesis 28:15:

   Psalm 23:4:

   Psalm 34:18:

   Psalm 73:23:

   John 14:16–18:

For reflection: When have you allowed your feelings to overrule the truth about God's presence with you and His love for you?

4. Sometimes, in the difficult times, I become independent in trying to take care of myself rather than fully depending on God. Have you ever done this, and if so, what was the result?

Thankfully, God is very patient. While He knows His way is better, He just continues to love us until we come to our senses. Psalm 86:15 assures us that God is _____ ___ _____, and that He has an abundance of _____ love and faithfulness. Psalm 136:26 again assures us that His _____ _____ will last forever.

5. Have you ever sacrificed moments of joy because you were too busy to recognize them for what they were? What price do we pay when we do so?

What does Proverbs 8:17 have to say about that?

How much does God delight in us according to Zephaniah 3:17?

6. God ministered to me through Isaiah 30:20–21 (NLT): "Though the Lord gave you adversity for food and suffering for drink, he will still be with you to teach you. You will see your teacher with your own eyes. Your own ears will hear him. Right behind you a voice will say, 'This is the way you should go,' whether to the right or to the left." How does that encourage you?

For reflection: When have you experienced God teaching you through adversity? Or guiding you back to the right path?

7. Have you ever stayed busy to avoid dealing with your pain or to shield yourself from hurt or from future hurt? It's really just a way of trying to stay in control rather than surrendering our control to Him. God repeatedly tells us there is another way to cope with the hard times in life. What answer does He give in each of the following verses?

Psalm 9:9:

Psalm 20:1:

Psalm 46:1:

Psalm 62:8:

For reflection: Will you take refuge in Him to heal the pain now? Tell Him what pain you need Him to heal.

8. Sometimes we use busyness as a shield to prevent feeling pain. Other times it is used to impress people or to live up to others' expectations of us. The enemy will often tempt us with things to keep us busy and distracted in order to kill our peace, cause us to become bitter and resentful, and keep us from being effective in the calling God has for us. God's economy is always different from ours, and His way is usually so much simpler.

In Luke 10:41–42, we are advised that we tend to worry about _____ things, but there is only _____ thing that is truly important. It all comes back to a matter of priority. Each and every one of us has enough time for what we make a priority.

For reflection: Have you ever come face-to-face with the truth that, "There comes a point when doing, achieving, and performing is no longer productive and is completely contrary to our heart's desire for peace"?[8] Describe that time.

9. Have you been in a place so desperate that, like me, you felt the pain was too much and you didn't know if you could hold on? I could not trust my own strength but had to depend on His. If you are reading this, you *did* survive. How did God meet you and your need?

    What encouragement are we given for just such times in Deuteronomy 4:29?

10. So many struggle with fleeting thoughts of, *Everyone would just be better off if I wasn't here* or even more serious suicidal ideations. What's crucial to remember is that *all* of these thoughts are not your thoughts—they are lies from the enemy! The enemy would like for us to give up, because he is threatened by God's great plans for our future. Repeatedly

in Scripture, God promises a hope-filled outcome if we will persevere. Record them here:

Deuteronomy 5:33:

Galatians 6:9:

James 1:12:

James 4:10 and 1 Peter 5:6:

For reflection: Maybe you've never had such extreme thoughts, but has the enemy ever tried to convince you that you were in some way a mistake or not essential to your family's life or to God's kingdom?

11. In our most difficult times, we all long to know we are not alone. What did God say about that in Genesis 2:18?

For reflection: How has God met that need for you during your difficult seasons?

12. We often put faith in the wrong things (our career, money, relationships, substances, busyness, etc.) to help us through painful circumstances. But God offers another way, a better way. What do the following verses say about God's better way?

Proverbs 3:5–6:

Matthew 6:23–33:

Matthew 11:28–30:

Ephesians 2:8:

For reflection: Has the enemy ever tempted you to cope with life's stressors in an unhealthy way? How did God show you that your coping style did not align with His truth?

13. Has the enemy ever tempted you to equate your worth or God's love for you with your accomplishments? How has this negatively impacted you when you weren't able to meet your goals or accomplish what you desired?

The enemy lies to us and tries to convince us we are unlovable or that God will withdraw His love because of how we feel or something we do. What truth does God give in the hope-filled promise of Romans 8:38–39?

And in 1 Corinthians 13:7?

Key Thoughts ⁓
- We may not feel it, but God is always with us.
- God's love is unfailing and doesn't depend on us.
- God's only requirement is that we believe.
- God's love is dependable and the only secure place to put our trust.

Your Rx ⁓

Record the following verses on index cards, recite them at least three times daily, and commit them to memory: Ephesians 3:17–18; Genesis 28:15; Psalm 136:1; and Romans 8:38–39.

Recommended Playlist ⁓

"God's Great Dance Floor," Chris Tomlin, © 2013 by sixstepsrecords/Sparrow Records

"Amazed," Jared Anderson, © 2006 by Integrity/Columbia

"One True God," Mark Harris, © 2007 by Ino/Columbia

"Multiplied," Need to Breathe, © 2014 by Atlantic Recording Corporation

Chapter 11

GOD USES YOUR PAIN

"Forget the former things; do not dwell on the past.
See, I am doing a new thing! Now it springs up, do you
not perceive it?"
Isaiah 43:18–19a

I like Job. At various times in my life, I have related to his seemingly relentless suffering. Yet I could only aspire to navigate the trials with such fortitude and grace as Job displayed. In waiting for God to intervene in his desperate times, in his humanness, Job began to struggle. He questioned the purpose for both his life and his suffering and wondered how much longer he would have to endure.

I appreciate the vulnerability and transparency with which Job shared with his trusted friends. While God considered him blameless and full of integrity, relentless suffering took its toll on Job. He had his limits. He had his doubts. He had his questions. And when he reached the end of himself, he even had his complaints. Through trials that would test any man, he didn't cave in to the peer pressure to curse or blame God, yet he was real and honest about the gravity of his suffering.

Our family has recently gone through a succession of difficult life circumstances, one right after another. Just in the past year, our family managed my twelve-week bout with pneumonia, an accident resulting in a concussion, staff turnover at my practice, and my husband's diagnosis and treatment of cancer. More than a couple people jokingly asked if I have felt like a "Jobette".

Recently, a friend delivered a meal to ease the stress of mealtime during chemotherapy week. As she set the meal down, she asked, "How are you two? I mean, really?" She paused, then continued, "I talk about you two all the time. As long as I've known you, almost twenty years, you've constantly inspired me with your faith, despite what gets thrown at you. You still have a smile on your face. What if this didn't happen for you or your faith, but for others' faith to grow? What if this isn't about you? What if it's about encouraging others through your own trials?"

What if, just like Job has been an inspiration to me, our suffering is an opportunity for us to inspire and encourage others? Wouldn't that just make the enemy mad, bring beauty for ashes, and give God all the glory?

God is not cruel. He weeps when we weep. He does not want to see His children suffer. I am convinced that because He promises to work all things together for our good (Rom. 8:28), He will use our pain for good, and encouraging others may just be one way He does that.

1. What is the hope-filled promise of Isaiah 43:18–19a?

2. In your own words, what work is required of us in 2 Corinthians 10:5?

    The Bible tells us to take *every* thought captive. We have 50,000 to 70,000 thoughts daily. How many of those thoughts do you think you are consciously taking captive? Do you think there is room for improvement?

3. According to Joshua 24:15, we have a decision to make. What is that decision?

    Serving God includes agreeing with His truth and not the enemy's lies. If we want God to do something new in our lives, we must first stop agreeing with the lies of the enemy and consciously choose to believe God's truth.

    For reflection: Is there an area in your life in which you want God to do something new? In what areas do you need to stop agreeing with the enemy and instead agree with God's truth?

#HopePrevails

4. A pastor of mine, Steve Dulin, once said, "Great faith comes from great victories and great victories come from great battles." When I was in the depth of my despair, I just wanted to know that something good would come out of it—that it wouldn't be for nothing.

   James 1:2–4 tells us part of the good that comes out of our trials we have.
   v. 2: An opportunity for _____.
   v. 3: When our faith is tested, _____ has a chance to grow.
   v. 4: When our endurance is fully developed, we will be mature and lack _____.

   For reflection: Have you ever been in such a difficult place you found yourself thinking that if you just knew something good would result, it would be worth it, or you could make it?

5. Sometimes God uses our pain for our own good, rather than for the good of others. According to Psalm 119:71 and 2 Corinthians 1:8–10, what is the valuable lesson He may use our pain to teach us?

6. Romans 12:1–2 (MSG) encourages us: "Don't become so well-adjusted to your culture that you fit into it without even thinking." How often do you think we try to fit in because we wear a mask rather than letting others see our faults and relate to our pain? What would it take for this to change so that we could heed Paul's admonition?

7. In Isaiah 61:3, God promises to give us beauty for ashes, joy for our despair. But we can forfeit those blessings if we run from Him and His work in us rather than trusting Him to bring us through.

   For reflection: Have you ever forfeited such blessings because of running from God and His work in you in the painful times in your life?

8. David cried out to God in Psalm 70:1. Record his words here:

   "God never protects us from that which He will use to perfect us."[9]

For reflection: Have you gone through difficult experiences from which you would have preferred to be rescued, but God used them instead to better you? In what ways are you thankful for them now?

9. When I was going through the valley of depression, it would have helped to have knownsomeone else who understood what I was dealing with. There is power in the words, "Me, too." Even when no one else can, Jesus offers that. How does Isaiah 53:3 describe Him?

Because of the pain I endured, I now have a deeper compassion, which allows me to relate to others going through similar trials.

For reflection: Has God ever given you an opportunity to relate to another person's suffering that you wouldn't have been able to if it had not been for your own experiences?

10. We're in a war against the enemy of our souls, the very one who seeks to steal our joy, kill our peace, and destroy our identity. What does the Bible promise in Genesis 50:20?

God has allowed me to minister to others using my story so that they know they aren't alone and that someone understands. Don't you know that this makes the enemy mad?

For reflection: How have you seen God use something for good in your own life that the enemy intended to harm you?

Key Thoughts

- God doesn't waste our pain.
- Depression will change us, but that can be a good thing if it increases our faith and draws us closer to God.
- What the enemy intended for harm, God will use for good in our lives to bless both us and others.

Your Rx

Record the following verses on index cards, recite them at least three times daily, and commit them to memory: Isaiah 43:18–19; 2 Corinthians 10:5; and Psalm 119:71.

Recommended Playlist ⌐

"Set the World on Fire," Britt Nicole, © 2007 by Sparrow Records

"Even When It Hurts," Hillsong, © 2015 by Hillsong Church T/A Hillsong Music Australia

"Clean," Natalie Grant, © 2015 by Curb Records, Inc.

"Oceans (Where Feet May Fail)," Hillsong United, © 2013 by Hillsong Church T/A Hillsong Music Australia

Chapter 12

THE WAY TO HOPE

Dear friend, I hope all is well with you and that you are as
healthy in body as you are strong in spirit.
3 John 1:2 (NLT)

I had just delivered my address to a room packed full of
women in their spring skirts and capris. While they all looked
cute and put together, as I looked into their eyes one by one
when they spoke to me afterward, I saw the pain and shame.
I had shared my story, so they knew I could relate. I had said,
"Me, too." But I didn't stop there. I shared how I successfully
traversed that valley to get to the other side.

Isn't that what we really want? We don't just want to hear
someone say, "I made it, you can, too!" We want to know, "And
this is how . . ."

"Would you pray for me?" they asked, one after another.
But one especially tugged my heart. She went on to say, "I've

been depressed for years, and I feel so angry. I've been taking my medicine, and I tried counseling for a while. I eat pretty well and exercise most days, but it just doesn't get better. I almost didn't come tonight. I rarely go to church anymore, and I just don't feel like reading my Bible or praying."

Her story wasn't unlike those I hear from many I meet and in some respects, not completely unlike my own.

When it darkened my own life, I felt such shame, because as the doctor who had treated depression for decades, I thought I should've had the knowledge to prevent it. And when I tried all the same treatments I had recommended to my patients (sleep, diet, exercise, medication, therapy, etc.) and it still wasn't enough, I felt like a fraud. Until . . .

Until God showed me that we cannot ignore caring for our spiritual health and addressing the spiritual roots of disease. Things like being in God's presence, prayer, knowing God's Word, understanding what it means to "take every thought captive," practicing gratitude and thanksgiving, and offering praise and worship—*that* made all the difference then, and it still does today. The spiritual aspect of treatment is perhaps the most important, yet sadly it's the part that is too often missing and the reason many don't experience the change they seek. "We can make our plans, but the LORD determines our steps" (Prov. 16:9 NLT).

1. What is the hope for all of us found in 3 John 1:2?

2. What important question did Jesus ask in John 5:6?

   Why do you think Jesus asked the lame man that?

   For reflection: If He asked you the same question, what do you think it would entail, and how would you answer?

3. One of the most important ways to treat depression is to watch your thoughts and words. What is the warning given in Proverbs 4:23?

4. We have anywhere between 50,000 to 70,000 thoughts per day. What is the admonition we are given in 2 Corinthians 10:5?

5. Proverbs 4:23, which we read in wuestion number 3 warned us to guard our hearts. Why is this so important, according to Luke 6:45?

6. Read Matthew 15:11–20. What does Jesus say about the importance of the words we speak?

7. Matthew 15:11 says that it is the things that come out of a person's mouth that defile them. Our emotions are the outward manifestation of the thoughts and beliefs we have and the words we say.

    For reflection: In what area of your life do you struggle most with your thoughts and words?

8. To bring our thoughts into alignment with God's, as we are called to do in 2 Corinthians 10:5, we must first know God's Word. According to John 8:32, what is the blessing of knowing His Word?

9. While the Bible doesn't specifically reference therapy per se as a treatment component for healing, what does it tell us in the following verses about wise counsel?

Proverbs 12:15:

Proverbs 19:20:

1 Corinthians 12:7:

10. What does the Bible have to say about taking care of your temple in the following verses?

1 Corinthians 6:19–20:

1 Corinthians 10:31:

1 Corinthians 3:16–17:

11. What does the Bible have to say about sleep and rest in the following verses?

Psalm 3:5:

Psalm 4:8:

Psalm 127:2:

Proverbs 3:24:

12. With respect to taking care of your temple, in which area—rest, nutrition, exercise, or socialization—do you struggle with the most and why?

For reflection: In which area will you commit to making an immediate improvement?

13. In Luke 8:43–48, why was the woman with the issue of blood a perfect example of the importance of making sure that being in God's presence is a priority?

What benefits do the following verses give for spending time in God's presence?

Psalm 21:6:

Isaiah 26:3:

James 4:8:

For reflection: In what ways do you find yourself consciously or unconsciously sacrificing time in God's presence, and what subsequent impact has this had on your life?

14. What do the following verses tell us about the importance of regularly spending time in God's Word as part of our healing from, as well as protection against, depression?

Psalm 107:20:

John 8:31–32:

Ephesians 6:11–17:

Romans 12:2:

Proverbs 4:4–5:

15. Scripture says that God's Word has the power to heal, so it is crucial that we are anchored in it. The Bible also says that faith comes by hearing, so when we recite His Word out loud, we increase our own faith. We also give God freedom to work in our lives by agreeing with what He has already declared to be true.

For reflection: How does the enemy distract you from spending time in the Word?

In what ways can you improve the degree to which you intentionally anchor yourself in His Word?

16. The Scriptures give us many reasons why prayer is an essential component of any treatment plan for healing from depression.

In John 16:24, Jesus encouraged us to pray so that

_____.

In Psalm 138:3, David reminds us that in return for our prayers, God offers _____.

According to Philippians 4:6–7, when we pray, tell God our needs, and thank Him for all He has done, then we will experience _____.

Hebrews 4:16 indicates that when we approach God in prayer, we will receive _____ and find _____

_____

_____.

17. The Scriptures encourage us to pray about everything. Yet often, when we most need to pray, we least feel like it, let alone surrendering our needs, wants, and ways of doing things to His perfect plan.

For reflection: Compare a time in your life when you were struggling but you stayed steadfast in your prayers to a time when you didn't. What difference did it make? What impacted your willingness to stay consistent in your prayer life or not?

18. According to the following Scriptures, what role does obedience to God play in our healing journey?

Psalm 40:8:

Psalm 34:9–10:

1 Samuel 15:22:

For reflection: In what areas has God been speaking to your heart recently and calling you into greater obedience to His ways?

19. What can we learn about the role of praise and gratitude in our healing from Habakkuk 3:17–19?

From David in Psalm 37:23–24?

From Paul in Philippians 4:4–7?

For reflection: The Bible gives us numerous examples of men who, despite their dire circumstances, continued to offer praise and gratitude to God. David taught us that God replenishes the joy of those who intentionally praise and thank Him. How can you be more intentional in your praise offerings to God despite your circumstances?

20. If we want to rid ourselves of depression, we must choose to trust God. Given that the Scriptures indicate that when we choose to trust God we will not be disappointed, why would we not trust Him?

In what areas do you need to more fully trust God today?

Key Thoughts

- We take the responsibility to actively participate in our own healing.
- We must be careful of our thoughts and words, taking them captive.
- Taking care of our temple is essential.
- It is also crucial to care for our spirit.

Your Rx

Record the following verses on index cards, recite them at least three times daily, and commit them to memory: 3 John 1:2; Proverbs 4:23; Romans 12:2; and Psalm 37:23–24.

Recommended Playlist

"In the Sanctuary," Vicki Yohe, © 2005 by EMI Gospel/Pure Springs

"Closer," Bethel Music & Steffany Frizzell Gretzinger, © 2014 by Bethel Music

"Nothing Is Impossible," Planetshakers, © 2011 by Integrity/Columbia

"Come to the Mountain," Mark Harris, © 2007 by Ino/Columbia

YOU HAVE A GIFT TO GIVE

Praise be to the God and Father of our Lord Jesus Christ,
the Father of compassion
and the God of all comfort, who comforts us in all our
troubles, so that we can comfort those in any trouble,
with the comfort we ourselves receive from God.
2 Corinthians 1:3–4

She walked into my office, her infant over her shoulder, infant carrier slung over one elbow, and her diaper bag over the other elbow. A pacifier hanging from a robin's-egg-blue ribbon dangled from her clenched teeth.

"How can I help you?" I offered.

"Would you mind taking him for a second while I get set-tled?" she managed to ask.

"Would I mind? I thought you'd never offer! There's noth-ing better than snuggling a newborn baby."

"Correction . . . a *sleeping* newborn baby!" she replied as she transferred her sweet baby boy to my arms, then started to disentangle herself from all the trappings of her new experience of motherhood.

I helped her get settled and comfortable. As I offered the precious bundle back to her, she waved him back to me. I readily consented with my smile and took my seat in front of her. I gave her a couple of moments and quietly watched as she took a few deep breaths.

"How are you?" I asked.

That was all it took for the floodgates to open and the tears to begin flowing. I stood, picked up the box of tissues from the side table with my free hand, and set them down next to her. She looked up at me through her tears. That look told me everything I needed to know.

I recognized her: I had been her almost twenty years ago. On the outside, everything was wonderful: My pregnancy had gone perfectly, labor and delivery went well, and I had what I believed to be the perfect baby. Yet I was not okay. Even when the baby was not crying, I was . . . all the time . . . over anything, over nothing. It made no sense. At least not to me.

Her voice cracked as she barely whispered the words, "What's wrong with me?"

I remembered wondering the same thing. Here I had what I'd always wanted, a sweet baby boy, a loving husband, a beautiful home, and yet anyone who could see me behind my closed doors would think I was anything but happy because I cried all the time. Everything seemed like an effort. I didn't want to do anything or see anyone. I felt like a failure. Wasn't this supposed to be the happiest time of my life? I constantly wondered, *What is wrong with me?* Surely others could see through my masked exterior and wondered the same thing. I had watched the mom and baby shows on the TLC channel . . . I didn't resemble any of them. Maybe I wasn't cut out for motherhood after all. Maybe God had made a mistake.

"Oh, sweet girl, this isn't your fault. There isn't anything wrong with you. I know what's going on," I assured her.

"You do?" she looked up through hair that had fallen over her face as she sobbed, a small glimmer of hope finally returning to her tearstained, reddened eyes.

I remembered feeling that glimmer of hope, too. My mother had called one evening to check on me and the baby. "How are you?" she asked. Just as it happened in my office with this sweet new mom, her question made me sob. It took me a few moments to regain my composure before I could explain what had been happening and my fear that I was somehow losing my mind. "Sweetheart, I think you've got postpartum depression. Put your husband on the phone." She explained her suspicions to my husband and made him promise that as soon as we hung up, he would call my doctor and ask for help. I didn't need to suffer any longer.

And having gone through it myself and being a doctor trained in mental health issues, I was then able to assure this new mother that she did not need to suffer any longer, either. Consistent with Scripture, I could comfort with the comfort I had been given.

As our time together ended and I helped her regather all her mommy gear, she asked if she could give me a hug. As I released her, she relayed, "I feel hopeful for the first time in weeks. I feel like you just gave me my life back. Thank you."

"You don't have to thank me. When you come out on the other side of this, and you will, you'll be in the position to do that for another young mom someday. You will have a gift to give someone else: the gift of compassion and empathy that comes from your own experience. That'll be thanks enough."

1. What is the hope-filled promise of 2 Corinthians 1:3–4?

2. For reflection: You now know that it is God's desire for you to be in health, but it is the enemy's tactic to lie to you in order to steal, kill, and destroy. What is the greatest truth you have learned through these pages that you will continue to stand on?

3. Because we have suffered and been comforted, we have a gift to give others—the very same comfort that we have been given. How can *you* use *your* experiences to comfort others?

4. In helping others, how do you think it might help you in your own continued healing journey?

Key Thoughts ⌒

- God wants us to comfort others with the comfort we have been given.
- It's God's desire for us to be in health physically, mentally, emotionally, and spiritually.
- You now have tools to fight depression from a spiritual perspective and you can offer them to others.

Your Rx ⌒

Record 2 Corinthians 1:3–4 on an index card, recite it at least three times daily, and commit it to memory.

Recommended Playlist ⌒

"Living in Your Freedom," Gateway Devotions, © 2014 by Gateway Create Publishing

"Thank You, God, for Saving Me," Chris Tomlin, © 2013 by sixstepsrecords/Sparrow Records

"With Every Act of Love," Jason Gray, © 2014 by Centricity Music

"I Will," Citizen Way, © 2016 by Fair Trade Services

HOW TO HELP A
DEPRESSED LOVED ONE

When Job's three friends . . . heard about all the troubles
that had come upon him, they set out from their homes
and met together by agreement to go and sympathize with
him and comfort him.

Job 2:11

I grew up in a home with a mother who, sadly, suffered
from depression most of my childhood. Back then, I didn't
have a label for it other than, "That's just the way she is." Not
having yet experienced depression myself, I had limited understanding of the pain she endured or how to best help or
support her.

Fast-forward several years: I married one of the most emotionally even-keeled men you'd ever be blessed to meet. Depression did not tend to run in his family, nor had he ever
suffered in its valley. Yet he did suffer his own pain and torment

when his wife went down under it and he could neither relate to it nor understand how to help her through it.

Trying to explain depression to someone who has never suffered from it is a bit like trying to explain what a rainbow looks like to someone who has never been able to see. The good news is that just as you don't have to have suffered from cancer to help others with a cancer diagnosis, you don't have to have gone through depression to help others who are suffering. Scripture gives us the keys.

1. According to Job 2:11, what did Job's three friends do for him?

2. According to Galatians 6:2, what are we called to do?

   What is one way to do this, according to Romans 12:15?

3. According to Ephesians 4:32 and Colossians 3:2, what should the attitude of our heart be?

4. Given what you now know about depression, how can you best help someone who struggles with it?

Key Thoughts ⟶

- There are things you can do to help a depressed loved one.
- Being present is more important than saying the right words or doing the right thing.
- Even when you don't understand, have a heart of compassion.

Your Rx ⟶

Record the following verses on index cards, recite them at least three times daily, and commit them to memory: Galatians 6:2; Romans 12:15; and Ephesians 4:32.

Additional Resources ⟶

I recognize that those who suffer with depression are not the only ones who struggle. Friends, family members, and co-workers struggle to appropriately support him or her, especially when they themselves have never walked through depression's dark door and do not fully understand. Caring for a depressed loved one is a dance requiring that we learn how to love them in the midst of it while they learn how to cope with it.

I've written a free resource for you entitled, "How to Help a Depressed Loved One." It's available on my website, http://DrMichelleBengtson.com/how-to-help-a-depressed-loved-one-chapter. There you will also find related blog posts (e.g., "10 Things to Know If You Have a Depressed Loved One," or "What to Say If You Have a Depressed Loved One") and resources to support you during this time. I also have a weekly column, "Ask Dr. B," where I address reader-submitted questions so I can address the topics of concern to you.

CLOSING PRAYER

Dear heavenly Father,
I thank You that we can trust You to be true to
Your Word. I thank You that You promise
never to leave us or give up on us.
I thank You that when we hurt, You hurt.
I thank You that You have sent the
Holy Spirit to comfort us in our times
of heartache and trouble. I thank You that
You have promised to give us a crown
of beauty for ashes, a joyous blessing
for mourning, and praise instead of despair.
I thank You for the healing work that You
have begun in this precious one's heart and soul,
and I thank You that You will be true to Your Word,
which says that You who have begun a good work

in this one will be faithful to complete it.
Finish Your good work so that this one can in
turn comfort others with the comfort
they have received.
In Jesus' name I pray, amen.

LEADER'S GUIDE

Depression is hard, and there wouldn't be such a stigma surrounding it if there wasn't so much shame. We know that shame doesn't come from God, but from the enemy of our souls. The last thing we want to do individually or in a group setting is to convey any shame, blame, guilt, or condemnation. What participants need is grace, mercy, acceptance, compassion, and love.

Be sure to emphasize the importance of maintaining confidentiality within the group so that members feel safe to share sensitive matters without fear that their personal information will be talked about outside the group.

Begin each session with prayer, asking that God would lead the session, and that He would use the time to help break the chains that have kept people bound for far too long. As you begin each session, review the Scriptures from the "Your Rx" section and recite them out loud as a group. As you end each session, encourage participantsnot only to do the work in the next chapter, but also to commit to memorizing the Scriptures suggested in the "Your Rx" section.

You may want to consider covering the material in the introduction, "When the Whole World Is Laughing but You," and "A Letter to My Depressed Self" during an introductory week when participants get to know each other a little bit and share what brought them to this part of their journey.

To guide you in reviewing the material from each chapter, answers to some of the non-reflective questions follow.

When the Whole World Is Laughing but You

1. Encourage the group to come up with one to three benefits of trying to get rid of depression.
2. Encourage them to define *hope* in their own words. If they can't come up with anything, perhaps offer *H*aving *O*nly *P*ositive *E*xpectations.

As you close this week, remind them of the key thought that they are not alone. Even when they feel alone, there are others who understand. And even when they can't identify others who understand, God does, and He promises to never leave them alone.

A Letter to My Depressed Self

1. We often treat others kinder and gentler than we treat ourselves. Urge each member of your group to write an encouraging letter to their depressed "friend," but then to read it back to their own depressed self with the same love and kindness they would offer to someone else.
2. God is for us, and that's the most important thing for us to remember. He will meet all our needs. He is our Helper.
3. prosper, harm, future, and hope. God has a plan for each of us and it is good; it includes a future and a hope!

As you close, encourage group members that God is 100 percent for them and wants to meet their every need. Depression is not a punishment from Him. Rather, His plans for them are good and include a future and a hope. Encourage them to hold on to Jeremiah 29:11 in the difficult days.

Chapter 1 – This Thing Called Depression

1. If we don't know what to look for, it can impede our ability to seek help.
3. David expressed his depression in the psalms: "Why, my soul, are you downcast? Why so disturbed within me?" Encourage the group to describe their experiences with depression in their own words.

4. "For reflection" questions are intended to challenge the reader to think about how the material applies in his/her own situation.

5. If one in four Americans experience depression at some point in their lives, discuss the expected incidence just within the room alone. That means there is nothing to be embarrassed about, because depression is a very common cause for concern.

6. Discuss known or suspected barriers to people getting assistance for depression.

7. Ask if respondents were surprised by the number of endorsed symptoms. Had they ever considered those signs to be symptoms of depression before?

8/9 Psalm 31:7: unfailing love; Psalm 33:20: He is our help, Psalm 34:17–18: helper/rescuer; Psalm 54:4: helper/sustainer; and Hebrews 13:6: helper; We're not alone. Repeatedly in Scripture, God is referred to as our Helper.

As you close, reinforce that we hurt ourselves by being uninformed and that often people don't recognize depression for what it is. But by getting education, help can follow. God wants to be our help!

Encourage the memorization of the verses mentioned in the chapter prescription ("Your Rx"). Explain that faith comes by hearing and that reciting verses out loud can help in the memorization process and also foster one's faith.

Chapter 2 – You Are Not Alone

1. God promised that we are not alone.
2. Christians sometimes hide their pain from each other out of fear of being judged, criticized, or rejected. Even within the Church, problems (including depression) are often attributed to too much sin or not enough prayer in one's life—that's a blame game that promotes shame and condemnation that isn't from God.
3. Discuss the encouraging promises. See what other scriptural promises they find encouraging.
4. How do group members react to hearing the phrase "be very glad" in the Scriptures? Discuss the notion of having the wonderful joy of seeing His glory.
5. Discuss the difference between situations when shared Scriptures are encouraging and helpful and the times when they aren't.
6. Tears are safe here. God promises to collect all our tears and ultimately to dry them.
7. What's the significance of Jesus' question to the lame man who was waiting for his healing? Encourage discussion about why those who are depressed might *not* want to really get well.
8. Reinforce that they are not their depression, and that God does not shame anyone for going through depression.
9. Discuss the gift offered common to all three verses.

As you close, reinforce that they are not alone despite how they may feel. Encourage them to understand that God is with them and cares about their pain. He doesn't shame us. He wants to comfort, teach, and heal us.

Encourage the memorization of the Scriptures suggested in "Your Rx."

Chapter 3 – The Underlying Causes of Depression

1. Scripture clearly reveals that we have an enemy in the dark world who is responsible for most of our suffering.
2. Encourage discussion about when they have been successful in praising and giving thanks even when it seemed difficult and what they experienced as a result.
3. From their own experience, how would they contrast the results from asking, "Why?" versus "What do we do about it?" or "How do we cope with it?"
4. Considering the impact of our thoughts on our brain chemistry and hence our mood, how do they respond to 2 Corinthians 10:5?
5. There is no truth in him; for he is a liar; the father of lies. Discuss what makes it difficult to identify the enemy's lies, and why it's so difficult to ignore his lies and believe God's truth instead.
6. The idea that their thoughts are not their own but are actually from the enemy may be a new concept to them. Take the time to explore the idea that our thoughts come either from the Holy Spirit or from an evil spirit.
10. What are ways in which we can "resist the devil"?

11. Review the different potential contributors to depression and have each participant discuss which ones they can identify at work in their own lives.

13. the spirit of fear; power, love, and sound mind. Many who struggle with depression also struggle at least to some degree with fear/worry/anxiety. Discuss what impact this has had on their lives.

15. Explore what other scriptural truths they can come up with to refute the common lies they battle.

16. How comfortable are they knowing what God says about them in His Word?

17. No weapon that is formed against you will prosper.

As you close, review that there are different contributors to depression, but ignoring the spiritual aspect is too often the reason more people aren't effectively treated. We must recognize that our thoughts influence our physical and mental health and then pay attention to where those thoughts come from.

Chapter 4 – Recognize That You Have an Enemy

1. Jesus promised: "I have come that they may have life, and have it to the full."

2. Encourage them to think of a hope-filled promise from Scripture that has meant a lot to them.

3. When they've been depressed, how have they been different from their non-depressed selves?

4. God's power is displayed perfectly when we are weak.

5. Because we can't be perfect, God sent Jesus to pay for our imperfection on the cross. Now when God looks at us, He sees us as He sees Jesus.
8. The captives will be released, prisoners will be freed, the time of the Lord's favor has come. To all who mourn in Israel, He will give a crown of beauty for ashes, a joyous blessing instead of mourning, festive praise instead of despair. In their righteousness, they will be like great oaks.
9. God doesn't blame, shame, or condemn.
10. It is guaranteed that we will go through difficult times, but God promises that He will be with us and that we will make it through.
14. Even when the enemy intends to harm us, God will use it all for good.

As you close, remind them of the importance of recognizing that we have an enemy who lies and wants us to focus on our feelings rather than on God's truth.

Chapter 5 – Recover Your Joy

1. Those who sow in tears will reap with songs of joy.
2. Trials cause our faith to strengthen and our endurance to grow, so that we come out stronger than we were before.
3. You will have the wonderful joy of seeing His glory when it is revealed, but in Isaiah He promised to restore the crushed spirit of the humble and revive the courage of those with repentant hearts.

4. Encourage them to share from personal experience.

6. Psalm 86:15: compassionate, gracious, slow to anger, faithful
   Job 19:25: redeemer
   Romans 8:32: provider
   Ephesians 1:7–8: kind, wise, understanding

7. As we trust in Him, then we will be filled with joy and peace.

8. Be in God's presence.

11. Prayer—asking in Jesus' name.

13. Sacrificing a thank offering may mean different things to different people, but for one who is depressed it might mean something as little as going to church even when you don't feel like it, just to thank God for what He has done for you in the past. Explore other ideas with your group.

14. When we get busy comparing ourselves to others, we stop being thankful for what God is doing or has done in our own life because we focus on what we prefer in others' lives.

15. Explore the concept that we are what we think in our heart.

As you close, emphasize that one of the enemy's main tactics to get us or keep us depressed is to steal our joy. We often lose our joy by focusing on ourselves rather than on God. Have the group brainstorm ways that they can refocus their attention on God instead this week.

Chapter 6 – Reclaim Your Peace

1. He will be with us and give us His peace.
2. Encourage discussion about what peace is like to them.
3. *Yahweh-Shalom* (Peace)
4. Comes from God/Jesus as a gift from Him
5. 1. Don't worry.
   2. Pray about everything.
   3. Tell God what you need.
   4. Thank Him for all He has done.
6. Matthew 6:25; 6:30–33; and 1 Peter 5:7: God will give us what we need because He cares for us.
7. Trust God completely.
10. Discuss what makes it difficult to think of ourselves in positive terms.
11. Romans 8:1: There is no condemnation/guilt for those who belong to Christ Jesus.
    Ephesians 1:9; Colossians 1:13–14; and 1 John 2:12: He purchased our freedom and forgave our sins.
    Ephesians 4:24 and 2 Corinthians 5:21: Jesus made us righteous.
    Isaiah 43:1: God paid the price for us and called us by name. We are His.
    1 Corinthians 15:57: Jesus' death gave us victory over sin and death.
13. Numbers 11:10–15   Moses
    Ruth 1:13, 20–21   Naomi
    1 Samuel 1:7–10   Hannah
    1 Samuel 16:14–23   King Saul

1 Samuel 30:4-6   David
1 Kings 19: 4–5   Elijah
Job 30:16–26   Job
Jonah 4:1–9   Jonah
2 Corinthians 1:8–10 Paul
Matthew 26:38; Luke 22:41, 44; John 11:35 Jesus
Isaiah 26:3: Trusting God and staying focused on Him.
Philippians 4:13: Relying on His strength, not our own.
14. Trouble
15. Sometimes it's hardest to forgive ourselves, but Christ already did. Encourage a time of prayer for God to reveal any area where they need to forgive themselves with His help.
16. Take every thought captive to make it align with what Scripture says.
17. Life to the full.

As you close, reinforce that a second way the enemy seeks to make us and keep us depressed is by killing our peace. Anxiety is the absence of peace, and worry comes from believing lies from our enemy. We lose our peace by focusing on ourselves and our problems. So if we want to reclaim our peace, we must focus on and trust God, the Solver of our problems.

Chapter 7 – Reestablish Your Identity

1. You belong to God; the Spirit who lives in you is greater than the spirit who lives in the world.
2. "Really?"

5. I am fearfully and wonderfully made; we are God's masterpiece.
6. We belong to God—that's where our identity is established.
7. We are His children.
8. Our words can: praise or curse, bring death or life.
9. 1. created; good 2. plan; good 3. good Bonus: good
10. Ephesians 1:7 and Colossians 1:14 say He purchased our freedom and forgave our sins.
12. all, each of us, all
    Romans 3:23 We've all sinned and fallen short of the glory of God.
    Colossians 2:13 God made you alive with Christ, for He forgave all our sins.
13. Jeremiah 29:11 God has plans to prosper you and not to harm you, plans to give you hope and a future.
    Philippians 1:6 He who began the good work within you, will continue His work until it is finally finished.
14. You are beautiful. (Ps. 45:11)
    You are victorious/more than a conqueror. (Rom. 8:37)
    You are loved forever. (Jer. 31:3)
    You are Christ's friend. (John 15:15)
    You are seated with Him. (Eph. 2:6)
    You are the apple of His eye/His most treasured possession. (Zech. 2:8)
    You are holy and dearly loved. (Col. 3:12)
    You are valuable. (Matt. 6:26)
    He forgave you. (Ps. 103:12)
    He persistently seeks you. (Luke 19:10)

As you close, emphasize that the enemy seeks to destroy our identity, but our identity as loved children of God is good.

Chapter 8 – Know Your Worth

1. God ransomed us. He called us by name; we are His.
3. He gives and loves freely.
4. 1. He adopted you. (Eph. 1:5)
   2. He formed you. (Isa. 43:1)
   3. He called you His. (Ps. 95:7; Ps. 100:3; Isa. 43:1)
5. To lay down one's life for one's friends.
6. We have true freedom when God sets us free.
7. Genesis 50:20a God will use for good what the enemy intended for our harm.
   Romans 8:28 If we love God, He will cause everything to work together for good.
8. Isaiah 49:16 We are so important to God that He engraved us on the palms of His hands. Isaiah 62:3 God loves us so much that He will hold us in His hand and put us on display. Song of Solomon 4:9 We have captured God's heart. Ephesians 1:5–7 God adopted us into His own family.

As you close, review the exercise suggesting they place a dot in the center of their palm daily for a week. God thought we were worth so much it that His Son died for us. God adopted us into His family. He chose us to be part of His family.

Chapter 9 – Remember Your Secure Destiny

1. No one can snatch us out of the Father's hand.
2. Encourage discussion about how we tend to live based on the lie that our past predicts our future, when the truth is, our destiny is secure despite our sin if we have received salvation and the forgiveness through Jesus.
3. Discuss how we often think God is going to respond compared to how we have seen Him actually respond in the past.
4. 1. d Moses (Exodus 4:1–13:)   a. Self-pity
    2. a David (Psalm 13:1–6:)   b. Inferiority
    3. e Naomi (Ruth 1:20–21:)   c. Fear of failure
    4. b Zacchaeus (Luke 19:1–7:)   d. Self-doubt
    5. f Martha (Luke 10:38–42:)   e. Abandonment
    6. c The Hebrew people (Num. 13:26–31) f. Drivenness
5. Christ made us righteous and freed us from the penalty for our sins.
6. v. 1 bind up, freedom, release

    v. 2 comfort

    v. 3 crown of beauty, oil of joy, garment of praise

    v. 6 priests, ministers, wealth

    v. 7 double portion, inheritance, double portion, everlasting joy
7. Romans 8:37: We are more than conquerors.

    Philippians 4:13: I can do everything through Christ, who gives me strength.

    1 Corinthians 15:57: He gives us victory over sin and death.

2 Corinthians 2:14 He uses us to spread the knowledge of Christ everywhere.

8. 2 Timothy 1:7a (KJV): "For <u>God</u> hath not given us the <u>spirit</u> of fear:"

Ephesians 6:12 (KJV) "For we wrestle not against <u>flesh</u> and <u>blood</u>, but against <u>principalities</u>, against <u>powers</u>, against the <u>rulers</u> of the <u>darkness</u> of this world, against <u>spiritual wickedness</u> in high places."

2 Timothy 1:7b: He gives us power, love, and a sound mind.

9. It was by faith that even Sarah was able to have a child.

The boy's father exclaimed, "I do believe; help me overcome my unbelief."

10. Matthew 6:27: Worrying won't add a single hour to our lives (but it might decrease them)!

1 Peter 5:7: Give our worries to God.

11. He always gives us a way out of temptation.

As you close, remind them that their past does not predict their future—God does. Their destiny is secure with Him when they have accepted Jesus as their Savior. If any are there who have not done so, offer to show them how. Guide them through the basic plan of salvation with Romans 3:23: Romans 6:23: Romans 5:8: Ephesians 2:8–9: and Romans 10:9–10.

Chapter 10 – Be Confident That Nothing Separates You from God's Love

1. When Christ lives in our hearts, God's love grows and strengthens us.
2. God loves us in all our imperfections, and because He loves us that much, He sent Jesus to die for us. We don't have to hide behind a mask.
3. We are never alone; God is always with us.
4. Psalm 86:15: assures us that God is compassionate and gracious; His love is unfailing.
   Psalm 136:26: His faithful/steadfast/everlasting love will last forever.
5. Proverbs 8:17: He loves those who love Him, and He won't hide Himself from those who want to find Him.
   Zephaniah 3:17: He loves us so much, He sings about us.
7. Consistently, He tells us that He is our refuge.
8. many; one
9. Deuteronomy 4:29: When we take the time and effort to search for God, we will find Him.
10. Deuteronomy 5:33: Obey God, so that you may live and prosper and prolong your days.
    Galatians 6:9: We will reap a harvest of blessing if we don't give up.
    James 1:12: God blesses those who patiently endure.
    James 4:10: and 1 Peter 5:6: When we humble ourselves before God, He lifts us up and honors us.
11. Genesis 2:18: It was not good for man to be alone.
12. Proverbs 3:5–6: Trust God to guide your path.

Matthew 6:23–33: Don't worry, but instead put God and His kingdom first, and He will give you everything you need.

Matthew 11:28–30: Follow God's way, which is not heavy or difficult.

Ephesians 2:8: God saved us by His grace—there's nothing we can do to earn this free gift.

13. Romans 8:38–39: Nothing can ever separate us from God's love.

1 Corinthians 13:7: God's love won't give up on us.

As you close, emphasize that despite our feelings, nothing can ever separate us from God's love. His love is unfailing and doesn't depend on us. All He asks of us is that we believe in Him.

Chapter 11 – God Uses Your Pain

1. God is doing a new thing in your life.
2. We must pay attention to our thoughts and make sure they are in line with what God says in His Word. If they are not, we must reject them and replace them with His truth.
3. We must make a choice for ourselves whom we are going to serve.
4. v. 2 joy
   v. 3 perseverance
   v. 4 nothing
5. Suffering teaches us to pay attention to God's teaching and rely on Him.

9. He was despised and rejected—a man of sorrows, acquainted with deepest grief.
10. The enemy intended to harm you, but God will use everything for good.

As you close, emphasize that God doesn't waste our pain. Even in the case of depression, at the very least God will use it to change us and draw us closer to Him.

Chapter 12 – The Way to Hope

1. God wants us to be in good health.
2. Do you want to get well? Explore why Jesus would ask what seems to be an obvious question.
4. Guard your heart.
5. Take every thought captive and make sure it lines up with what the Word of God says.
6. What you say and do reflects what is in your heart.
7. It's the words we speak that defile us.
9. We will be set free by the truth of His Word.
10. Wise people seek wise counsel and don't rely on their own opinions.
11. Our body is not our own to do with what we want—we honor God by taking care of our body.
12. God gives us rest for our own good and will watch over us while we sleep. She received her healing by having faith and being in His presence.
Psalm 21:6: eternal blessings, joy

Isaiah 26:3: perfect peace

James 4:8: God will come close to you

14. Psalm 107:20: His Word healed them.

John 8:31–32: Jesus said that the truth of His teachings would set people free.

Ephesians 6:11–17: If we put on God's armor, we will be able to stand firm against all strategies of the devil; we will be able to resist the enemy in the time of evil.

Romans 12:2: "Be transformed by the renewing of your mind. Then you will be able to test and approve what God's will is."

Proverbs 4:4–5: If we follow God's commands, we will live long and gain wisdom and good judgment.

16. John 16:24 Our joy will be complete; we will have joy.

Psalm 138:3: strength

Philippians 4:6–7: His peace

Hebrews 4:16: mercy; grace to help us in our time of need

18. God is more pleased with our obedience than He is our sacrifice. With obedience comes joy and His provision for all that we need.

19. Habakkuk 3:17–19: Even in times of trial, rejoice and praise God because He is always worthy.

Psalm 37:23–24: Trust that God will direct your steps, and praise Him for His trustworthiness.

Philippians 4:4–7: Praise, rejoicing, and thanksgiving come before God's provision, healing, and peace.

As you close, reinforce that, just like the lame man had to pick up his mat and walk, we must desire to get well and then actively participate in our healing. We must carefully choose our thoughts and words to make sure they are consistent with God's truth. Taking care of our temple is essential for good emotional health. We must also care for our spirit by being in God's Word, being in God's presence, praying, praising, worshiping, and having a grateful heart.

You Have a Gift to Give

1. God will first comfort us, then we will be able to comfort others with that same comfort He gave us.
2. Encourage discussion regarding the most helpful truth they have learned in this study on which they will stand during the difficult days ahead.
3. Encourage discussion about how even if they aren't all the way out of the valley yet, they are further along than someone else they will encounter. Have them discuss ways they might be able to help others in need of their experience and comfort. How can they essentially say, "Me, too!" in a way that will help pull someone out of the valley rather than climbing back down into the valley with them?
4. How can they see ways in which helping others can further help them in their own healing journey?

As you close, remind them that God wants us to be healthy physically, mentally, emotionally, and spiritually. He has given us the tools. Now He wants us to comfort others just as we've been comforted during our difficult times.

Encourage them to continue memorizing the "Your Rx" Scriptures as their defense against the lies of the enemy.

How to Help a Depressed Loved One

1. Job's friends traveled from their homes to comfort and console him.
2. Galatians 6:2: Share each other's burdens.
   Romans 12:15: Be happy with those who are happy and weep with those who weep.
3. Kind and compassionate
4. Encourage discussion of practical ways to help others who are struggling with of depression. Ask the participants what has helped them in the past. What hasn't?

As you close, remind the group that it isn't necessarily their job to know the right words or the perfect thing to do to help someone who is going through a difficult trial. Sometimes just being present with a kind and compassionate heart is the best gift you can give.

Encourage participants to avail themselves of the free resources listed at the end of this chapter.

NOTES

1 Dr. Michelle Bengtson, *Hope Prevails: Insights from a Doctor's Personal Journey through Depression* (Grand Rapids, MI: Revell, 2016), 19–24.

2 Author unknown.

3 Bengtson, *Hope Prevails*, 75.

4 Bengtson, *Hope Prevails*, 99.

5 Bengtson, *Hope Prevails*, 108.

6 https://www.goodreads.com/quotes/230453-define-yourself-radically-as-one-beloved-by-god-this-is.

7 http://www.goodreads.com/quotes/641961-what-we-know-matters-but-who-we-are-matters- more.

8 Bengtson, *Hope Prevails*, 154.

9 Bengtson, *Hope Prevails*, 164.

CONTACT INFORMATION

Dr. Michelle Bengtson is a speaker and the author of *Hope Prevails: Insights from a Doctor's Personal Journey through Depression.* She is a board-certified clinical neuropsychologist with over twenty-five years of professional expertise in the diagnosis and treatment of medical and emotional disorders. She is also a wife, mother, and friend. As she trusted God to carry her through her own personal trials, she discovered that hope prevails. To help relieve the sufferings of others in the middle of their storms, she offers sound, practical tools; affirms worth; and encourages faith by offering hope as a key to unlock joy and relief.

Dr. Bengtson earned her PhD at Nova Southeastern University. She lives in the Dallas/Fort Worth area with her husband of over thirty years, their two sons, and two dogs. When she isn't seeing patients in her private practice or speaking words of hope and encouragement to groups around the country, you'll likely find her out on the water, where she is most at peace.

Contact Information:

For more hope, stay connected with Dr. Bengtson at:
Website: http://www.DrMichelleBengtson.com
Blog: http://drmichellebengtson.com/category/blog/
Facebook: https://www.facebook.com/DrMichelleBengtson
Twitter: http://www.Twitter.com/DrMBengtson (@DrM-Bengtson)
LinkedIn: http://www.LinkedIn.com/in/DrMichelleBengtson
Google+:   http://www.google.com/+MichelleBengtson
Instagram: http://www.instagram.com/drmichellebengtson
Pinterest: http://www.Pinterest.com/Drbhopeprevails
YouTube: https://www.youtube.com/channel/UCn92D-HzGSZk8psDb2FKazOQ
Order *Hope Prevails*:   http://drmichellebengtson.com/hope-prevails-book/

ORDER INFORMATION

REDEMPTION PRESS

To order additional copies of this book, please visit
www.redemption-press.com.
Also available on Amazon.com and BarnesandNoble.com
Or by calling toll free 1-844-2REDEEM.